T0365603

Quiet Horizon

Releasing Ideology and Embracing Self-Knowledge

Greg Jemsek

Order this book online at www.trafford.com
or email orders@trafford.com

Most Trafford titles are also available at major online book retailers.

Note for Librarians: A cataloguing record for this book is available from Library
and Archives Canada at www.collectionscanada.ca/amicus/index-e.html

http://www.quiethorizon.com

Printed in Canada and the United States.

ISBN: 978-1-4269-1127-9 (sc)
ISBN: 978-1-4269-1128-6 (hc)
ISBN: 978-1-4269-1129-3 (e)

Trafford rev. 01/20/2011

 www.trafford.com

North America & international
toll-free: 1 888 232 4444 (USA & Canada)
phone: 250 383 6864 ♦ fax: 812 355 4082

For my sons
Misha and Sam

Contents

Contents

Acknowledgements

The idea for this book originated in the many engaging discussions I had in the 1980s with my friend, Peter Nelson. Peter, those talks helped me understand how important a commitment to self-knowledge is and what a razor's edge we all walk on when we choose to pursue it.

I'd also like to thank Max Clayton for accepting my "proposal" to review the book. The spirit of your workshops, Max, reminds me of much of what I'm trying to communicate here about direct experience.

To Greg MacDonald - "Greg B" - thanks for your review of the manuscript and especially for your encouragement in the 80s to teach a university course on "New Religious Movements." Teaching that course got some of the wheels turning over in my mind about how ideologies work.

Finally, to my partner Sahni - this book and our relationship began at the same time, so I'm sure we'll both enjoy seeing see what life is like without me writing all the time. We get that chance because your support, encouragement, and patience have all been indispensable in getting me across the finish line - thank you, dear one.

Introduction

How does a person today live a meaningful life, as opposed to just a successful one?

How does he nourish spirit and self-knowledge in a world characterized by fractured community, relentless mobility, obsession with consumption and the diminishing value placed on healthy relationships?

How does he learn to trust his own inner compass for ultimate guidance rather than the theories and systems put forward by experts and ideological organizations, both religious and secular?

When I was 10 years old, such questions were the furthest thing from my mind. The realms of philosophy, religion, phenomenology, psychology, or any other discipline devoted to self-knowledge were light years from my awareness, buried under the usual concerns of growing up. Later that year – in the wake of a powerful, unsolicited mystical experience – the seeds of these and similar questions were planted in my consciousness. They were planted by the demand this experience made on me to wake up and pay attention. I was too young to really know what to do with such an imperative, but that didn't matter. The aftershock of the experience wasn't going anywhere. It never strayed far from my awareness, biding its time until I was old enough to begin a confused and often ill-fated attempt to figure out what to do with it.

I don't know if such "accidental illuminations" happen to everyone. I do know that in the aftermath of my encounter, the importance of self-knowledge exploded onto my radar – and has taken up permanent residence there ever since. The first chapter of this book describes the event I experienced that made this the case.

Such an event might seem like some sort of blessing, or cosmic good luck, or some other version of divine fortuitousness. Indeed it felt like that at the time. Any sense of specialness I may have permitted myself, however, was quickly overridden by the angst I generated in the years that followed: years where I made one foolish decision after another as I tried in vain to reproduce this experience. Decisions that showed how easy it is to fall right off the road, even when you think you know where you were going. Decisions that found no protection in good intentions, or in the counsel of others; that confused and befuddled me when I had hoped they would do the opposite.

One particular cluster of events – a three year period when I joined, devoted myself to, and then left a socio-spiritual organization in the 1970s – was particularly important in helping me clarify what leads to self-knowledge and what doesn't. The organization I joined is not the centerpiece of this discussion. It is the backdrop against which I began, in earnest, a long and confusing process of coming to terms with an awareness that often felt bigger than I could handle, was impossible to express, and which wove itself through the psychological issues of my life in ways I found perplexingly difficult to untangle. This book, in other words, details what I've learned about the pursuit of self-knowledge by examining the confusing and treacherous terrain that opened up in front of me the moment I recognized I was living on the surface of life rather than in the heart of it.

Why write a book about such matters? This question plagued me enough to delay its start for many years. My first concern was that it would be read as another "cult expose" from a bygone era no longer relevant to today's world. I questioned the value of connecting, as I attempt to do in the pages that follow, the events of a three year period in the mid-70's to the way ideologies operate in contemporary society. I knew that the urgency I felt then would be foreign to many readers unless a real connection with the present could be made.

My second concern was that I would find it impossible to avoid putting forward remedies to the situation that would either repeat what has already been more eloquently stated or would not be relevant to anyone beyond myself. Why write a book if it's not putting forward something new, or something helpful?

Both those hesitancies were overcome when the central issue explored here – the difficulty of pursuing self-knowledge without attaching one's self to an ideology – reappeared in my married life in the 1990s. This contributed to the end of my 17 year marriage, followed by the tragic suicide of the woman I had for so long viewed as my life's partner four years later. That sequence of events was dramatically influenced by ideological thinking, and gave tremendous urgency to my desire to write about the earlier experiences I had had wrestling with how such thinking shapes a human life. In doing so, I hope that this book will offer numerous points of identification to anyone committed to furthering his self-knowledge without compromising his sovereignty in the process of doing so. A large part of the argument I make here is that whether doing so privately or publicly, alternatively or in the mainstream, in a spiritual context or a secular one, anyone who seeks to genuinely broaden his awareness and pursue a more authentic existence will, at some point, run into the straitjackets imposed on his efforts by ideological approaches. How is a person to navigate through this?

The urgency of this question, in combination with my own experience, repeatedly took me back to the particularly but-not-exclusively American tendency to embrace ideological solutions to life's problems. I have lived in two other countries for extended periods of time since the events portrayed in this book (8 years in New Zealand and 10 in Australia) and it strikes me repeatedly that while the issues discussed here can show up anywhere, it is in the United States where they are taken to extraordinary extremes. Since the time of frontier settlement, the U.S. has embraced ideology and "expertness" in ways that have led to extreme forms of evangelical exuberance. This exuberance frequently leads a person away from, rather than towards, the truth of his experience.

Such was the case for me until the rigidity and authoritarianism inherent in ideological approaches – combined with the memory of my mystical experience – prompted me to live my life based on my own inner knowing rather than on someone else's prescriptions. Looking back at how I moved myself to this point led me to see how influential my experience in the 70s had been, and how relevant its lessons currently are. That relevance stems from the naiveté and hopefulness of that era. It was a time when ideological dramas played themselves out more nakedly, in less complicated ways. A time when the innocence of youth combined with the often awkward, unprofessional beginnings of ideological organizations of the era laid bare dynamics underpinning the whole effort. That straightforwardness operated outside of the fog incessantly manufactured by the now much more sophisticated influence industry – a fog embedded in the nervous system of any ideology, obscuring its intentions by thrusting forward promises of perfection. Promises that serve as the public face of the organization. On the other side of this fog the past can be seen for the useful warning bell of the future that it is. Particularly now, when more people seem to be willing to acknowledge the rush to apply ideological solutions as the overly simplistic and dangerous trend it is.

In writing this book it was important to me to encourage others interested in pursuing self-knowledge without embracing an ideology not to abandon their efforts. Some readers may have made mistakes similar to my own, and falsely concluded it was best to put their search to the side and just be "normal." I myself did this for many years. Tackling the increasingly onerous problems we as a society now confront, however, has taken away this option. It requires the efforts of everyone who understands the value of trusting his direct experience to pick up a shovel and begin digging. The speed and intensity with which ideological fortresses continue to be built urgently calls out for a contradictory effort.

The final reason for picking up my pen is the simple fact that I could not *avoid* writing this book. The reasons just given combined with the alarm I feel whenever I see the pursuit of self-knowledge waylaid by ideological – and increasingly fundamentalist – approaches still wakes me up at night. I concluded in one of these 2 a.m. moments that I might as well write about what I was thinking and see where it led.

The process of doing so has taken me into fascinating but messy territory. Simultaneously encouraging the search for self-knowledge without unknowingly veering off into a position where I'm suddenly legitimizing an ideological version of that quest is not as easy as it seems. The perplexing conundrum presented by all ideologies is the fact that their systems invariably contain valuable insights into life; insights we ignore at our peril. The issue is rarely one of philosophical content. It's the way carefully knit-together ideologies wrongly assume the mantle of being an absolute template for how everyone should live. The moment that step is taken, it is a short and usually unnoticed journey to pushing aside the freedom gained when people engage self-knowledge directly, unencumbered by external authority.

Why does a person relinquish that freedom so readily, even when it means sacrificing sovereignty over his life? To go as far as I could with this question, I've made every effort to stay close to my own experience: the events of my own life during the time leading up to, into, and out of my involvement with a socio-spiritual organization from 1973 to 1976. This book details how that involvement pushed me to view any effort to portray life as a predictable affair with a more penetrating gaze; to see how thoroughly ideological approaches have been normalized in American society.

Coming to this conclusion required examining my personal experience through the lens of the psychological, sociological, cultural and transpersonal factors that have shaped the pursuit of self-knowledge in the U.S. then and now. This included looking at the frequently ignored question of how a person relates to the vulnerability so essential if he is to access a more panoramic awareness. The underside of vulnerability has always been the way it increases a person's susceptibility to influence by, and conversion to, ideological prescriptions for living. This susceptibility is no less prevalent now than it was in the period I explore in this book.

I realized as the writing of this book unfolded that confusion regarding both the value and dangers of vulnerability was at the heart of my anxiety about ideology. In my own life and in that of many people whose paths I have crossed, I have seen how the psychological vulnerability underpinning a person's surreptitious imaginings about the benefits of collapsing into the seemingly benevolent arms of an ideology all too frequently tills the soil which allow various forms of fundamentalism to be planted. Ideology is not the same thing as fundamentalism, but the difference is one of degree, not of kind. Both are predicated on the desire to eradicate uncomfortable feelings of doubt. This desire can drive a person towards conversion to many different kinds of ideologies. He may tell himself, at the beginning, that this is simply the process of adopting a viewpoint. Isn't adopting a viewpoint necessary if he is to connect his values and beliefs to his behavior? What he may not recognize is that he will be prompted to adopt much more than this once the guardians of that viewpoint enlist him in their efforts to extend their influence more widely. Once that happens, he is in a position to verify one of the central insights uncovered by Philip Zimbardo in his dramatic simulated prison experiment at Stanford University in 1971: that values are shaped by behavior, much more so than the other way around. What a person does is what matters. Consequently, what may begin innocently enough as an intellectual exercise can turn ever so quickly into a behavioral march that converts curiosity into compliance and freedom into obedience. Yes, adopting a viewpoint is certainly not the same as becoming an ideologue or a fundamentalist – but the gap between these categories is surprisingly small and often crossed without a person knowing he has done so.

What *does* distinguish a person adopting a viewpoint from one who embraces an ideology? How does the incremental relinquishing of sovereignty over one's life occur during the conversion process? Where does the power of belief, and its impact on living, fit in? What are the social lures that convince people to take on board an ideology when they may have an initial reluctance to do so? What are some of the bedrock narratives that underpin American society's view of itself and pave the way for adopting ideologies? How does the intensity of a truly transcendent moment serve to bend a person in the direction of an ideology? What does the reality of pursuing self-knowledge in the face of persuasive ideological forces require in this day and age?

Questions such as these are at the heart of this book. They are the questions ideologies ignore. Ideological organizations prefer to offer universal systems of living and thinking meant to prevent such queries from even arising. Their success in doing so is based partially on their ability to conflate the notion of self-knowledge with the various "salvation" promises they offer: enlightenment, endless prosperity, complete egalitarianism, permanent freedom from suffering, heaven, paradise, and the like. The ultimate truths they sell us. This distorts and overrides the quieter curiosity and enduring rigor required for genuine self-inquiry. What may begin for a person as a sincere effort to behave decently, live genuinely, and satisfy a need to contribute to the larger society gets shouted down by certainty promises and time-consuming disciplines. The breadth, complexity, and hard work associated with addressing questions of self-knowledge is sidestepped, replaced with seductive promises of perfection: if only the seeker will turn his life over to experts and authorities who claim to have more of a grip on that life than he does himself. In a world where people are increasingly overwhelmed by the complexities of living, this is a powerful attraction.

The problem with deciding to adopt an ideology in lieu of the uncertainty involved in seeking self-knowledge directly is straightforward: once a person starts ignoring his awareness, he begins the process of compromising his sovereignty. This involves a disempowering of both his conscience and his ethical sense. The parts of his life he lives secretly grow larger, allowing self-interest and fear to gain a firmer foothold in his psyche. It doesn't look like he is "selling his soul" in the dramatic way depicted by playwrights. Nonetheless it adds up to that, bit by bit. The personal insecurity that leads to such decisions, the cultural narratives that support it, the surrogate communities that lull the person into thinking it's all right are all mistakes I have personally made. I have tried to put all of them under the microscope in this book. I have done this because they are all things I continue to see people doing on a daily basis everywhere, in both secular and religious organizations.

I was surprised by how strongly the ethical dimension of all this emerged the deeper I explored the topic of ideological commitment. I refer in particular to the responsibility each of us takes for his own awareness. Taking that responsibility seriously brings forward ethical qualities that humanize a person in ways that nothing else can. Those who do so ultimately move beyond self-interest to a recognition of their interconnectedness with others. That recognition serves to awaken a person's ethical sense still further. It can be argued that it puts a person in spiritual territory. I believe it does, and in doing so, place this book outside of the many excellent writings that have emerged in recent years critical of fundamentalism but also of religious sentiment altogether.

In other words, my experiences with ideology have not led me to dismiss the incredible need for spiritual awareness many such ideologies spring from in the first place. It is the distortions that follow such experiences that trouble me. Distortions that are just as prevalent in secular ideologies, a fact easily forgotten in the current day focus on religious fundamentalism. That focus frequently leads to knee jerk reactions that place fundamentalists into the category of

"other," a mistake of fear conveniently ignoring the susceptibility to ideology we all face in a world becoming more
complex with each passing day. It's a susceptibility which,
ironically, often has its origins in a sincere desire for greater
self-knowledge.

Nourishing that desire in non-ideological ways is the
perplexing task confronting us all.

Chapter 1

The Narrowing of God

"Self-surrender to something or someone who appears more powerful than the individual's weak ego or will is an essential feature of conversion."

- Antony Storr

"Faith is always coveted most and needed most urgently where will is lacking; for will, as the affect of command, is the decisive sign of sovereignty and strength. In other words, the less one knows how to command, the more urgently one covets someone who commands, who commands severely - a god, a prince, class, physician, father confessor, dogma, or party conscience."

- Freiderich Nietzsche

It started 37 years ago when I decided to attend a free lecture on meditation.

Free things were always a bonus to a university student, but I probably would have gone even if there had been a charge. I was interested in learning about this mysterious eastern import that was supposed to bring such peace and calm.

When I walked through the door of the classroom where the talk was scheduled, I felt as though I had just been dropped inside Aladdin's lamp. Smoke was wafting through the air from some exotic incense. Vases of flowers were spread throughout the room. On the floor in the front there was a small table, covered by an ochre colored Indian cloth with a complex, repeating pattern – elephants, or monkeys, maybe both. On top of this was another vase of flowers, a lit candle, a small bell hanging from a stand of some sort and, most interestingly, a picture.

The picture was of a man dressed in some kind of faded orange gown, similar in style to the kind people wear in hospitals. He didn't have much hair. The man's eyes had a strange foggy look, as though he had taken some sort of medication. I had no idea who he was.

It wasn't until I took my seat in the small student desk that I paid attention to the speaker for the evening. He had on a gown too, but it was very white. He also had a short haircut, unusual for a young person at the time, and a string of brown beads around his neck. His eyes looked a bit funny too. I concentrated on those eyes for most of the talk. He kept rolling them to the heavens when he'd want to emphasize something. Frankly, I was a bit worried he might tip over backwards. He kept on his feet though, and spoke a lot about the peace that had come into his life as a result of learning to meditate from his guru, Sri Chinmoy.

He did seem very peaceful. After the talk was over I approached the front to pick up some literature about his group and, for some reason, I found it difficult to raise my head to meet his eyes for more than a brief second. It was strange; I felt as though I'd walked into some kind of bubble. It wasn't a bad feeling, though. It felt simultaneously safe, contained, and expansive in all directions. I hadn't felt like that in a long time. Since I'd been 10 years old, in fact.

That was when I was growing up in the Chicago suburb of Western Springs. On the particular day I was remembering, a girl I had a crush on had rebuffed my attentions during a school field trip. That was all the trigger I needed to remind me of another, more serious rejection, six years earlier. On that occasion my mother had put me on an airplane, saying she'd be right back, and then exited my life through the fuselage door. I must have sensed at the time there was a betrayal in progress, because I shattered any tranquility that might have existed on the plane before that moment with the full brunt of my four year old rage. That fury continued to live inside me when I arrived in Chicago for my new life, this time with my father and, about two years later, a stepmother. Neither of them made the necessary effort to explain my mother's abandonment of myself and my sister, preferring instead to pretend she didn't exist. The incident at school as a 10 year old brought back the emotions of her desertion, and the insecurities associated with it flooded to the surface and overwhelmed me.

I decided that day I needed to get some answers. Even though the only thing I remembered about my mother was that she lived in Texas, I ran away from my Illinois home that day to track her down: to find out why she had left my sister and myself. I had 90 cents in my possession, and immediately spent it on a large package of candy – Milk Duds, which I knew lasted a long time – and hit the road.

Shortly into my journey, I came up to an ugly, dark creek I had to cross, running alongside the busy TriState freeway. The creek seemed impossible to cross - not physically, but psychologically. It was as if I'd come up against some kind of imaginary "force field." The emotional chaos running inside me, however, lent me determination. I took off both shoes, threw them to the opposite side of the creek, walked through the water, put my shoes back on and, before too long, found myself in a neighborhood on the other side of the freeway. It was the first time I had gone beyond the imaginary boundary of my childhood territory.

Once I crossed that boundary, I found myself inside the proverbial looking glass. Everything around me was suddenly different. When I noticed the gentle breeze blowing through the oak trees lining the street, its movement was no longer just brushing my skin; it was infusing my entire body. Bits of sun penetrating the overhead canopy of leaves, lighting up patches of sidewalk, transformed into "doorways" I could travel through, giving me the feeling of navigating inside a kaleidoscope. Solid shapes dissolved into patterns of light and color, shifting with the wind and suffusing all my senses with peace and a profound sense of well being. As this occurred, any feeling of separation between the environment and myself melted away. I felt my whole body pulsing, moving and stationary at the same time, with no will of my own contributing to what was happening. The smells, sights and sounds of the moment exploded into a vividness greater than anything I had ever experienced; I found myself *becoming* those explosions. Any notion of having a body was replaced by a simple warm and glowing sensation, a sensation of disappearing: of merging into something much larger. I was suddenly in the center of what analytic psychotherapist Robert Johnson referred to as the "golden world," a phrase he came up with to describe the terrain of his own mystical experience. I had never felt so incredibly calm, and free, as I felt at that moment. Safe, contained, but expansive in all directions.

So I was surprised when, 10 years later in a University of California classroom, I was unexpectedly revisiting a touch of what seemed like this same feeling with a white-robed stranger who had just been rolling his eyes into his head while he talked and hadn't really said anything particularly stunning. Something about his presence had captured me, evoking that wonderful feeling from long ago.

What was this all about, anyway?

* * * *

As interesting as this question was eventually to become to me, it didn't cross my mind at the time. Instead, I accepted the feelings evoked by the Sri Chinmoy disciple's talk unreservedly, equating them with my experience as a 10 year old. The peace I felt in his presence was, in my mind, a version of the same thing.

I later realized this was wrong, seriously wrong. On the night of the talk, however, these two events merged in my mind. Unbeknownst to me, my numinous experience had forced open a doorway in my consciousness: a doorway that would unleash a string of memories, aspirations, and needs. I would spend years navigating through these trying, along the way, to understand their impact on my search for self-knowledge.

At the time, I simply felt extraordinarily different and, although I didn't yet know why, I was eager to find out. My youth, my psychological makeup and the memory of my mystical experience were combining to spur me on to continue my exploration. It was as though I'd unexpectedly come across a companion, someone whose presence was intimately familiar, someone I had known for a long time. That feeling was strange – I was only 20 years old and didn't know any flesh and blood people who even vaguely fit such a description – but it was accurate. I described it in a poem some years later.

When you are with me,
I travel the world
in the passenger car
of a holiday train,
rhythmically clicking,
through still life prairie landscapes
of grazing cows and cattail rivers,
winding easily through an auburn meadow.
I feel inside me
a twilight dance upon a solitary shoreline,
abandoned to the elemental orchestration
of brush stroke dunes
and surging ocean rainfall
leaping,
into a sun-kissed whirlpool
of whispering foam.

I meet your embrace
with the teary eyes
of a lost and fearful child
seeing outstretched before me
a garden of ten thousand lunar nights
a bed of fragrant lilies
sheltered by an ageless, silent shepherd
standing softly with his staff.

It is then that I watch
the yawning of my anger,
an ember slowly dying
in the living room fireplace,
tucked into its slumber like an exhausted athlete
after an all day summer football practice.

It is then
that the embarrassment of being myself
walks through a mirror of its own tenderness
emerging,
transformed,
an Arthurian page
clothed in the colorful raiment
of metamorphosis,
bearing the message of surrender.

When you are with me,
I can scarcely stand the freedom
so I sit,
in your mandala lap,
sharing secrets with you.

Clasping hands with your eternity
on our steady journey home.

My attention became fixated on this coming home feeling. I wasn't sure at the time what it was about, but I felt absolutely certain that doing whatever I could to reproduce my experience as a 10 year old was essential if I wanted to find out. I desperately wanted to recapture that extraordinary state of consciousness.

Although the power of that evening with the Sri Chinmoy disciple had stirred up this feeling, I chose to pursue all this with another group. I shopped around for an organization that matched what I considered to be key elements of what I wanted: meditation, an ethical approach, a nonwestern philosophical foundation, and a stance of social activism in the world. Before too long, I came across the group Ananda Marga, which means the *path of bliss*. Ananda Marga had all the components I was looking for, particularly social activism. That alone sharply distinguished it from other spiritual groups.

The internal shift I made during my venture into the spiritual supermarket was as important as my external decision. I came to see myself as a "seeker." That shift had leapt to the foreground of my awareness on the evening of the Sri Chinmoy talk, and the passage of time was making it stronger. It became part of an identity I steadily built up over the next two or three years. Over this period, being a seeker came to mean elevating self-knowledge to the highest possible level. What could I do to become a more aware person? How willing was I to take the necessary leaps into states of consciousness as powerful as the one I had already experienced? Career, relationships, and family fell off my priority list as this decision took root inside of me. I saw what Ananda Marga was offering as a golden opportunity to pursue what was most important to me with other people interested in doing the same thing. The excitement this prospect generated was enough to prompt me to leap across a number of extremely dubious cognitive bridges, and to do so with abandon. It was a leap into what I later realized was an ideological fortress; a leap made much easier by the steady stream of positive, and sometimes soaring, emotions that were now flowing through my life. A leap that persuaded me that adherence to Ananda Marga ideology was the surest, most direct way back to what I had experienced as a 10 year old.

Once I made this decision, I was amazed at the world that opened up in front of me: new friendships, new tools to learn about and use (yoga, meditation, eastern philosophy), a common language that I shared with others, and the sense that I could now respond positively and effectively to the materialistic, soulless, dehumanizing environment of mainstream America. I felt as though I had joined a group that included not just the members of Ananda Marga but anyone seriously pursuing spirituality. Spirituality, not religion – another distinction I was now making to separate myself further from the mainstream. The exotic nature of meditation, yoga, vegetarianism, and an activist social policy gave me the sense that I was doing something genuinely different, something that would deepen my self-knowledge while simultaneously allowing me to contribute to the world around me. Judging by the immediate emotional fulfillment, sense of aliveness, and excitement all my new activities were providing, it seemed clear that I'd made the right decision.

The mindset I've just described is that of a person walking down the path of conversion. A person who, for whatever reason, is planting new ideas in his life, doing what he can to get them to take root, experiencing tremendous excitement in the process, and willingly altering both his attitudes and his behavior to correspond to ideological directives. Conversion is, simply put, a *swoon*: every bit as intoxicating as falling in love is.

Despite how wonderful this all felt over the many months of my steadily growing engagement in Ananda Marga, conversion is never the absolute experience it is commonly portrayed as being. A part of my brain, from the start of my experience right to the end of it, was always suspicious of the encouragement I received from my teachers to "surrender my ego to something higher." Yes, this directive made sense in terms of what had already happened to me. Perhaps my reluctance was attributable to the fact that "something higher" was represented by an Indian railways accountant. That was the previous occupation of Ananda Marga's guru, a man named P.R. Sarkar, who was now in prison, charged (and acquitted some years later) with the murder of several Ananda Marga members who had left the organization. Perhaps it was because the guru I was supposed to obey was someone I had never even met. I'm not sure what my reluctance could be attributed to, but I lowered my head and kept trying to do as asked by Ananda Marga's *acharyas* (monks/teachers). My doubts at these beginning stages were small enough that this didn't present too big an obstacle. I settled myself down, tried to determine what surrendering my ego meant, and found myself riding the crest of an exhilarating wave. While I would never have agreed to a description of myself as converted at the time, I was certainly not thinking about turning back.

Not recognizing I was in an ongoing process of conversion was the first roadblock I faced at that time in my desire to advance my self-knowledge. It demonstrated how easily feelings of excitement, combined with tangible progress in life, can push aside uncomfortable, non-fitting dimensions of an experience: cultural foreignness, nagging questions about philosophy, or the strange ways people with authority in an organization sometimes act. All of these awkward elements fought for attention in my psyche but were, in these early days, losing the battle. I was committing, bit by bit, to shaping my behavior to see the world through the lens of this new ideology. I was steadily becoming secure in the belief that how things worked would now become clearer to me provided I followed, religiously, the dictates of the organization I had chosen.

This mindset resulted from the intersection of two powerful forces. The first was the genuine desire I had to repeat my mystical experience. That moment had been mine alone. It had come unsolicited. It had no association with anyone else, and it had occurred in a totally spontaneous, unanticipated way. It was by far the most powerful event of my life, a statement that remains true to this day, 48 years later.

The second force was also powerful, but in an entirely different way. It was the force of other people, impressively organized and committed to their philosophy, promising a return to this type of experience. Ananda Marga's teachers spoke continually in the voice of this promise. The end goal of enlightenment was just over the horizon, achievable by all. The fact that the organization attached the successful attainment of this goal to trusting their authority and ideology completely was, at this point, a minor concern. Everyone who had joined up was expending his energy aligning with the direction Ananda

Marga was heading. All of us were living, breathing, and speaking about it daily. There was no cynicism, just belief. Belief that the quickest and most reliable path to a transcendent reality was through ideological means.

Before too long, however, the unresolved tension in my awareness created by the demands of conversion began to regularly puncture my awareness. On the one hand, accepting Ananda Marga's perspective seemed to require absolving myself of responsibility for my life. How could I hand over the task of transforming myself to any authority other than my inner experience? Who could possibly know what path I was to travel better than myself? It challenged every notion I had of being an independent person.

On the other hand, there were times when the whole notion of conversion seemed not only harmless but essential to the act of transformation. How else was a person going to be able to let go of all the habitual and destructive ways of living adopted to fit in with mainstream society? Who, apart from a small minority of people, could withstand the constancy of that other form of persuasion: the relentless social pressure to conform to a life of materialistic striving, the grey suited normality that presses its demands for conformity on people every day? How was a person to avoid the erosion of conscience that accompanies *that* pact? These latter pressures seemed particularly insidious to me when I viewed them from the platform of my converted perspective. They seemed to have spawned a society that had abandoned its moral compass, succumbed to racism, violence, greed, and to a willingness of its leaders to do anything to retain power. How could an individual stand up to that alone? This was a thought I had carried with me before my conversion, and it had grown in strength. Wasn't it essential to join some group with an alternative vision and collectively craft a different sort of society, one that would head in a more enlightened direction?

My anger at U.S. society was strong, and joining Ananda Marga was giving me the opportunity to redirect it towards something I felt extremely positive about – yoga, meditation, vegetarianism, and spiritual community. All of these were clearly having a beneficial impact on my life. When you added to this my hope that involvement with Ananda Marga would ultimately take me back to the golden world, any resistance to the conversion methods employed by the organization evaporated. I had, after all, never felt happier in my life.

Pursuit of Ananda Marga's promises of a better life represented my first encounter with the overlap that exists between idealism and ideology. It's a tricky relationship to untangle, particularly because both have strong emotional undertones. When idealism is criticized, it's for a lack of realism: its imaginal dimension, its untethered relationship to pragmatic concerns. Pragmatism, on the other hand, is uninspiring at a minimum and, in the extreme, can have a dampening affect on hope. Ideologies look to blend these two by putting forward what its creators consider a pragmatic foundation for living strongly linked to hope.

Pursuing a life based on hope is universally important, but was particularly so for many young people growing up in the 60s in America. We had witnessed the power of hope generated by the Civil Rights movement. We had witnessed that power cross the racial divide and give courage to anti-Vietnam war protests. We were continuing to witness it through the ongoing explosion of cultural experimentation in every corner of the society. The rise of new liberation movements, including but not restricted to feminism and gay rights, raised the bar still further. The soaring oratory of people such as Mario Savio, Martin Luther King, Malcolm X, and Robert Kennedy sustained this momentum. It was an age where hope was on the ascendant, despite its frequent collisions with the despairing counter forces of assassination, the threat of nuclear extinction and a seemingly never-ending display of Machiavellian power plays in the political arena.

Hope was finding a warm welcome during this era inside the spiritual groups alighting on U.S. shores, its leaders giving talks wherever they could, its machinery organizing classes, retreats, and workshops while embracing all comers with open arms. Spiritual groups who asserted their differences from conventional religion - who aligned themselves with all the countercultural surges spontaneously appearing throughout U.S. society.

Hope has always been successful historically in persuading people to stoke the flames of their idealism. That persuasion frequently leads to taking one extra step, the ideological step, into conversion to a cause. Ideologies are an understandably attractive proposition in times where obvious social ills exist, particularly if that broader societal picture is combined with an individual life that could be considered unhappy, abusive, or simply neglectful. There were scores of young people in the baby boomer generation who viewed themselves this way, who saw their parent's vision of economic freedom as vapid, lifeless, and missing the entire point of living. The triggers for conversion were plentiful in American society at this time.

But was converting to something – even something that looked alternative, as Ananda Marga did to me in the early 70s – a way of advancing spirituality, or simply a way of relinquishing responsibility for it? Was I turning responsibility over to some higher authority so that the hard work I should be putting in was taken out of it?

These questions later became the second hurdle in my pursuit of self-knowledge, sitting alongside the reality of my conversion and prompting me to take a closer look. Both planted seeds of doubt deeper in my mind. It would still take some time before I was willing to relinquish the exhilarating ride I was taking on the wave of Ananda Marga's ideology, but the possibility of doing so began to circulate freely in my unconscious mind, right alongside my enthusiasm and commitment.

One thing doubt opened my eyes to immediately, however, was a stronger awareness of how widespread conversion tactics are. It became increasingly obvious that conversion was a universal phenomenon characterizing not just religious groups, but secular ones as well. Groups such as political movements, corporations, and the military. What did the conversion methodologies of fundamentalist Christianity, for instance, have in common with embracing Mao's communism, Amway's sales pyramids, or the patriotism found in the U.S. military's boot camps? Methods of conversion had always been applied anywhere a group of people gathered in an organized fashion and wanted allegiance to either their philosophy or their product. In secular environments, the nucleus of this effort is in advertising, sales, and marketing departments. The end such agencies are aiming for, however, is the same as it is in organized religion: to get people to form a bond with whatever their organization offers. Religious groups clearly want that bond to be longer lasting, to spread their philosophy deeply as well as broadly. Secular organizations have slicker, more heavily researched, and more psychologically subtle ways of persuading a person to get at least as far as the checkout counter. I noticed that these groups were starting to cross-pollinate. Fundamentalist groups were developing more refined images that embedded their intentions inside mainstream imagery more skillfully, and secular organizations started to experiment more with methods used by religious groups to encourage deeper commitment. Other traditional tools of religious conversion, such as an emphasis on a leader's charisma, the appearance of empathy for a potential convert's suffering, and the portrayal of a secure, all-knowing organization, also seemed to be crossing the religious/secular boundary. All of this reinforced the common underbelly I now saw in both approaches: their willingness to be predatory towards a person's doubts, insecurities and unhappiness.

I began to see what a huge problem all of this represented. One aspect of this problem, usually hidden to those on the receiving end of the conversion experience, was the simple fact that when a person is unhappy, he is much more easily influenced. His vulnerability makes him willing, out of mild or strong desperation, to believe someone persuading him, even if it means suspending common sense. Suspending common sense is much easier to do if a person feels alienated from his community, his family or...from himself. It's particularly easy to do if a person's identity has yet to take root, or if its development has veered off course. Especially if an attractive message promising to cure his ills or change his life direction comes along and invites him into its tent. This simple but devastating reality has been used by converting organizations for centuries as the foundation for increasing their numbers. I began to notice it working that way on me despite, or perhaps because of, the sincerity of my own seeking.

It was, however, more complicated than that. At the time of my attendance at the Sri Chinmoy talk, I was not consciously unhappy about anything. I had escaped my unhappy childhood years to what seemed to me to be paradise: California in the early 70s. I was enjoying my studies, making a few friends, and relishing the replacement of the flat, droning cornfields of Illinois with the vast, relaxed panorama of the Pacific Ocean. I had been moved enough by the Sri Chinmoy speaker to go out and join a spiritual organization of my own. I had shifted from a conventional existence to one that included meditating three times a day, doing yoga twice a day, eating vegetarian, and adhering to a moral code which, several months earlier, I never even knew existed. This all followed an internal logic I had taken to heart. Most importantly, I was associating the feelings I was now having with my mystical experience. I wouldn't have said I was seeking relief from my troubles. I would have said I was seeking a peace I had already briefly touched.

As my conversion trance deepened, I put such distinctions to the side. All the factors mentioned above – charisma, empathy, and the sense of expert knowledge – began to gush out of Ananda Marga's conversion spigot, packaged in a countercultural brand that held great appeal, and taking deeper root in my psyche. It was more than convincing enough for myself and many others to take the bait. Only later did I realize how much the success of the whole shadow play of conversion is facilitated when the intentions of the organization deploying it are hidden not just by them, but by the blindness to persuasion conversion swoons induce in their target audiences.

About 6 months into my involvement with Ananda Marga I began to consider, for the first time, whether the feelings I was having were really in the same arena as that wonderful sense of unity I had tapped into when I had run away from home. Could it be something else? When I considered that possibility, I began to suspect that this swoon had more to do with my emotions than I wanted to admit. Emotions connected to how I was defining myself, and how I viewed my role in the larger society. Despite the happiness I had with my life in California and the excitement my involvement in Ananda Marga had generated, I was beginning to drop below the surface more in my introspective moments. Meditation was clearly helping with this, as were the numerous conversations I had with others who, like myself, viewed themselves as seekers. I discovered in these conversations I was far from alone in the questions I was asking. Many people had confused emotions and unmet needs which seemed to go well beyond the expected developmental anguish of being 20 years old. Similar to myself, many I talked with also had an existential angst, a question of "What am I here for?" mixed into their personal turmoil. Encouraged by the culture of the times, seekers of all persuasions interested in self-knowledge were beginning to experiment with exploring the emotional potholes still unfilled in the road that had taken them this far. These potholes existed well below the threshold of personality. Because of the growing unease I felt about my own conversion, I concluded I needed to undertake a similar exploration if I was ever going to disentangle my psychological needs from my genuine interest in self-knowledge.

Despite this conclusion, the mixing of any emotional injury I was carrying inside myself with the golden world I had experienced earlier threw me into considerable confusion at the time. The line separating a psychological need from a spiritual yearning seemed a blurry one at best. It was clear that the success of converting organizations, religious and secular, depended on keeping that line out of focus. The sophistication of the emotional engineering they employed, their emphasis on both psychological vulnerability and spiritual yearning, and the never-ending pressure on people in the organization to continually act on behalf of the ideology all served to inhibit the reflection needed to sort through this process. This became even more challenging when the organization's efforts were promoted through the articulation of a convincing ideology, one that could rationalize its activities. All of this was thrown into the conversion blender, and the choice I and others made at the time was to drink it down.

Secular organizations in particular seemed to have already figured out the value in focusing on psychological vulnerability. They were clearly very adept at training their persuasion agents to entice customers to form an emotional bond based primarily on psychological need. That bond clearly wasn't with the product's performance. Presenting facts about how a product performed was becoming an almost extinct form of salesmanship. It had been replaced by psychological conversion strategies reliant, almost exclusively, on manipulating emotion.

When my university studies in sociology led me to read mid-twentieth century books deconstructing the advertising process – such as *The Hidden Persuaders* and *Subliminal Seduction* – I discovered how thoroughly people had researched this topic. These books first identified the advertising and marketing industry's passion for conversion through their illustrations of how each preys on unmet psychological need to entice people over to the cause of purchasing their product. Many years later I heard the phrase *desire priming*, regarding the cumulative affect of arousing desire, not for a specific product but generally, so that people are more likely to buy anything that will satisfy that desire.[1] The effectiveness of advertising and marketing strategies, combined with the vulnerability of youthful audiences, was implicitly acknowledged by the U.S. government during its clampdown on tobacco company advertising in the 90s. The rationale behind the government's proposed regulations had been common knowledge amongst the public for years. Would the combination of this knowledge and new laws be sufficient in blunting the effectiveness of the tobacco conversion campaigns? It was clear that the government had concluded that reason and education stood little chance against the advertising industry's seductive evocation of compelling imagery, and the only strategy that would have a chance of working would be an outright ban on targeting youth.

The adaptiveness and effectiveness of advertising campaigns advances all the time, and the linkage with emotional need has taken on increasing sophistication through newer techniques such as "metaphor marketing." This method, developed by Harvard polymath Jerry Zaltman[2], bases its approach on the well-understood fact that people think and react more powerfully to visual images than to words. The fifteenth century creators of the first Tarot decks knew this when they created their tool for prophecy and self-knowledge in northern Italy. It's the effectiveness rather than the novelty of this idea that is striking. Words play their part in evoking images, but the images themselves are the key motivating factor in determining what a person attaches to and, in the end, buys. Images connected to a sense of security, fear, sexuality and spirituality have all been researched by marketing agencies and folded into advertisements encouraging people to consume their way through life. The well-known result? Conversion through the allegiances each person forms with various brands, products, and companies; allegiances unconsciously linked to his own self-image and cemented through his purchases.

Religious group manipulation of potential converts seemed to prey on emotion in a different way. The primary distinction I noticed in their efforts was that as soon as a person indicated any allegiance whatsoever, he was asked to be active on the organization's behalf. I had only been in Ananda Marga a few months before I was asked to teach free yoga and meditation classes. Along with this, all the members of our local chapter were involved in social service projects of our own creation. Every week there was a group meditation ("dharma chakra,") and afterwards a business meeting to discuss the progress of social service projects already underway and new ones people could begin. There was nothing about this that felt insidious; it was simply a way of operationalizing the ideology – no different from methods employed in work places, trade unions, or advocacy groups. Doing so in combination with the daily spiritual practices I undertook, however, intensified these efforts and my identification with the ideology, the organization behind it, and the guru on top of it. Particularly when the payoff was not something as mundane as money, but the promise of permanent happiness. This served to put more layers of emotional commitment in place, a process secular organizations took notice of and began to mimic. A new question arose in my psyche, one that recognized my psychological vulnerability in all of this and asked: Were these layers of activity I was involved in with Ananda Marga healing the emotional wounds I carried, or taking advantage of them?

I began to notice other examples of emotional engineering occurring in the secular realm. Pyramid schemes were an obvious one, driven by their regular meetings honoring the top salespeople in an environment replete with corporate imagery, boisterous exuberance every time an old record was broken, and significant financial reward for those rising up the corporate food chain. Was it cryptic to even call this *engineering*? After all, weren't the parties involved simply boosting support for a common endeavor, and aren't similar methods employed in institutions large and small throughout society? Indeed they are, but my powerful experience of conversion was leading me to be increasingly less convinced that this was all harmless, even if it was considered normal.

Conversion seemed to progress through placing layers of commitment on top of each other. Reducing its influence in early stages could sometimes be addressed through bans designed to protect people, as in the case of the tobacco advertising regulations. The effectiveness of such an approach when it comes to dealing with people in later stages of commitment, however, seemed limited. If ideological commitment had penetrated to a point where a person knew what the situation was but either didn't want to do anything about it or felt he couldn't do anything about it, the situation was entirely different. I became much more interested in the role psychological vulnerability played in how converting organizations shifted people into these more entrenched stages. How did the emotional engineering of a group interact with a person's vulnerabilities to drive the embrace of ideology to deeper levels? What were the signs of this embrace?

One I was beginning to notice in myself was a passivity traveling underneath the busyness of my external life, both in Ananda Marga and at university. The initial relief I experienced at adopting an ideological focus, a relief based on having a ready explanation for things, was being replaced by a growing recognition that I was accepting an increasing number of things on faith rather than discovering them for myself. Furthermore, when I had experiences in the world, I was always interpreting those experiences through Ananda Marga's ideological lens, a self-imposed reinforcing of the conversion process. I wouldn't have framed it quite so clearly at the time, but by deceiving myself in this way I was moving in a direction opposite to my declared goal of self-knowledge. Self-deception and passivity clearly went against my desire to be a more aware person.

Why was I permitting this to happen? What characterized my emotional needs to prompt me to relinquish sovereignty over my life and replace it with obedience to organizational authority? Had it become so difficult to meet those needs in more traditional ways, i.e. through family love, support from community, or through a sense of belonging to a wider society?

Yes, it had. I had distanced myself from family deliberately because I felt there was no capacity there for sorting through the dramas I and other family members had lived through. I hadn't had time to establish community in California yet. As far as the wider society was concerned, I was angry at the direction it was heading, providing more than enough fuel for me to participate in any alternative I could find: anti-war protests, creating food cooperatives, helping to start free medical clinics, volunteering my time on the board of a community credit union, and any method I could think of to resist the "system." Was it any wonder how ripe I was for an organization that supported not only the spirit behind these protests, but a vision of how it could be different in the future?

When I thought about the issue more broadly, I suspected this backdrop of emotional need held true for many others of my generation. The exception seemed to be those who came from that rarest of beasts: a rock solid, supportive, healthy family. Were they immune to conversion? I concluded even they weren't if, like myself, a family member had experienced some form of mystical experience in life they wanted to replicate. That factor seemed at least as compelling as emotional need, and was fueling my drive to seek out more of the territory I had accidentally discovered.

The task in front of me now became identifying what those emotional needs were, how they had interacted with my brief immersion in the golden world, and how both had worked to increase my susceptibility to conversion. Starting with my emotional needs was essential because I suspected I had seriously underestimated their reach.

Perhaps understanding that better would help me disentangle those needs from my genuine spiritual aspirations, and to clarify the influence both factors had on my willingness to live ideologically.

1   "Spendshift", Fiona Carruthers, The Australian Financial Review Magazine, November 24, 2006
2   "Metaphor Marketing", Daniel Pink, Fast Company, May 1998.

Chapter 2

View from the Pool

"By its very nature, this sickness isolates us from one another and from reality, and it stands between us and all that we can hope to have and be. Its name is narcissism, and it lurks behind many of the social ills that plague twenty-first century America."

-Sandra Hotchkiss

The understanding I sought only emerged when I left Ananda Marga. After three years of intense involvement, I did exactly that. Once my head began to clear from the swoon I'd been in, I began to realize how much my psychological vulnerability had contributed to my susceptibility to conversion. In the past, I had overridden those vulnerabilities through employing a number of psychological strategies that had helped me function competently in my day-to-day affairs. Those strategies had protected me from directly addressing the painful realities of my mother's abandonment of me and the neglect and dysfunction I experienced in my subsequent family life. They were no longer necessary, however, and it soon became clear they were limiting my overall experience of life.

This had become apparent to me through my work as a psychotherapy client. That had given me a freshness of perspective that complemented my meditation practice in a number of ways. Examining life stories in the presence of an empathic and insightful listener helped me close the gap between the hurtful vulnerabilities those stories contained and the face of strength I presented to the world. Meditation served to solidify those insights and take the emotion out of the stories. I began to engage in a process of unwrapping the seemingly infinite strands of denial that had constricted me during my childhood years and early 20s, and found myself much more capable of directly experiencing the present.

My awareness of that denial became more acute when those explorations shifted from older life stories across to my days with Ananda Marga. When I focused on that time I realized, somewhat dishearteningly, how thoroughly *alive* I had felt during my first two years with the organization. My life had filled up with more energy, more purpose, and more calm. How was it that the unreal, trance state of ideological conversion – a denial of the outside world – had led me to such a positive frame of mind? I found this perplexing.

I eventually came to realize, however, that aliveness was not the most accurate way to describe what I had experienced. *Emotionalized excitement* was closer to the mark, and it had come at a cost. It had widened the gap between my private world – the one inside Ananda Marga and the public face I presented outside the organization. My sense of fulfillment had been in the former; my angst inhabited the latter. The price of sustaining my excitement was the compromise I made to my authenticity by living in this dual universe. The implication of that compromise was to move further away from trusting my inner compass – to turn instead to ideology for understanding how things worked. This pushed the two worlds further and further apart, necessitating either a deeper level of commitment to the ideology or a painful break away from it. This situation had arisen in part because of the way I had changed how I used, or didn't use, my intellect.

During my involvement with Ananda Marga, I had invested enormous amounts of energy into projecting my new found well-being to the world: through teaching its ideology in meditation and yoga classes, through engagement with community service projects, and through taking the initiative to be more involved at the international level of the organization. As I did all this, however, my enthusiasm had gradually given way to the nagging recognition that I was putting my critical faculties on hold. My wholehearted adoption of

Ananda Marga's ideology meant that each time I faced something new in the world – good news, bad news, new relationships, old ones – I began to automatically filter the experience through the lens of the ideology. If, for example, I received a refund check from the tax department during a time when our local group was attempting to launch a new social service project, rather than simply make a decision about whether to contribute this money or not to our new efforts, I first infused the event with meaning. I would think that the check must be some sort of confirmation that we were doing the will of the guru and the organization. This *magical thinking* began to puncture numerous experiences I had. Trust in myself was replaced by trust in ideological notions about how the world was constructed.

Additionally, I began using the occasion of any interaction with people outside the organization as an opportunity to persuade them to come to Ananda Marga events. While my enthusiasm was infectious enough to indeed bring more people into Ananda Marga's orbit, I came to see how it had confined me to reconstructing whatever I experienced through the filters of Ananda Marga ideology. Upon leaving the organization, I felt a deep sense of remorse about this self-deception, particularly the way I had used this energy to evangelize to the wider community. I had pushed that remorse away when I was still actively engaged by putting a mental boundary around what I later referred to as my "ideological zone." Every idea inside the boundary was not to be questioned, and every idea outside of it was to be reinterpreted.

This narrowing of intellect had other implications. My curiosity hadn't disappeared from view but it, too, began to funnel itself through these ideological filters. The excitement I initially felt was steadily replaced by pat answers to complicated issues. This certainty about things made it much easier to slide into intellectual laziness. Initially, I had placated my concerns about this by reminding myself that I was reading as much as I ever had, particularly books on spiritual philosophy. The content of those books, however, was confined to representations of viewpoints I was already advocating, and promoting, in my life.

All of this was, to some degree, natural to the beginning stages of engagement with anything new, especially as a 20 year old. Sustaining it over time, however, required a conscious effort. So did another compromise I made: between openness to experience and an uncritical acceptance of it. This shift occurred without my even noticing it. Whatever internal sentries were meant to be watching and warning me about mindless compliance had gone to sleep. It wasn't until I had filled a psychic suitcase full of unthinking nods to ideas I found objectionable that I finally awoke from this slumber. Not on one particular occasion but over time, as I found myself repeatedly jolted by the uncomfortable recognition that I had failed, on too many occasions, to act on my awareness and my values. To have done so would have meant generating something new, something contrary, the moment I began to feel intellectually stale or when my interpretations of events distanced me from the experience of them. To have acted in the world, not just inside my head. The number of times I could recall not doing so had put a significant dent in my self-regard.

These compromises hadn't settled into my life through any dramatic "crossover" experience; they had crept in through the back door, planting themselves bit by bit in my psyche. Only after I departed Ananda Marga and the swoon was put to rest did I again ask myself questions that were in alignment with my genuine aspirations for self-knowledge. Questions such as "Where had the intellectual growth that emerges from the struggle of ideas banging into each other gone? What about explorations that embrace curiosity, uncertainty, even anxiety? Why had I so easily given up being contentious in my thinking and turned instead to mollifying myself with ideas that offered me comfort instead?" The embarrassment I felt from retrospectively realizing these things was like a slap in the face.

If authenticity was one price I paid for my fundamentalist adventure, another was depth. Successfully ignoring the ever-widening gap between my inner compass and my Ananda Marga persona had required simplification of my worldview. Initially, this was a source of relief. Every time I titrated my daily life experiences through the cornerstone beliefs of Ananda Marga ideology, I felt an inner sense of certainty. I rested in this certainty, and took things no further than whatever piece of the Ananda Marga worldview most closely approximated whatever I was seeking to understand. In retrospect, of course, all of this seemed absurd, an obvious form of self-deception. Why would anyone engage in such folly?

Putting aside for the moment any of my own psychological failings that may have contributed to this behavior, the main reason I had persisted in compromising my intellect was more straightforward. It was because the emotionalized excitement my commitment to the organization had brought me was so rewarding. This excitement had brought me a freshness of spirit, a sense of certainty, a feeling of belonging, and a relief that diminished my usual ongoing worry and anxiety. My only reference point for such feelings was my mystical experience as a child. My desire for reproducing that state of consciousness had been so strong it had comfortably overwhelmed the quietly ringing alarm bells in my head.

This was easy in the beginning, because the benefits I was receiving were so powerful I had no desire to surrender them. The self-assurance I was discovering was creating a life infused with a dynamism that, apart from that venture into the golden world, I had never experienced before. I rode this wave strongly the first two years of my Ananda Marga experience before crashing, headfirst, into an accumulated reservoir of doubt. That doubt had begun as a small stream occasionally splashing the corners of my conscience; by the time I reached my final year, however, it was flooding my entire awareness.

In that final year the strength of my excitement, the oversimplifications it required, and the compromises to depth and authenticity I made all began to lose their hold on me. Ironically, this began to happen through the meditation process itself. When I meditated, both depth and authenticity returned, along with uncertainty, anxiety, doubt, and occasionally a moment or two of peace. Most importantly, meditation served to reconnect me with my inner compass. When I meditated, I felt no sense of compromise, no gap between inside and out. In addition, the calm that emerged from my meditations reconnected me to the experience of depth, and made me question what I found so alluring about what I was calling aliveness. It was after such experiences that I returned to the day-to-day world with questions about the values at the core of the Ananda Marga's ideology. Why, for instance, had the organization's guru supported the philosophy of Subash Chandra Bose, a contemporary of Mahatma Gandhi, who had felt that the best way to rid India of the British Raj back in the 1940s was through violence? What was the significance of the fact that Ananda Marga monks were willing to publicly self-immolate as a means of protesting the imprisonment of the guru?

Both these questions about violence confronted the nonviolence I considered foundational to my personal value system. That generated considerable anxiety, particularly the second question. It hit close to home because any of the Ananda Marga acharyas giving me spiritual lessons, some of whom I was quite fond of, might decide to take his own life to demonstrate his depth of spiritual commitment. Within Ananda Marga, particularly at the top of the organization, self-immolation was seen this way. I heard admiring talk of it regularly in my waning days with the organization, in 1975 when I had been asked to join the staff at the organization's world headquarters. Every time I heard these kinds of conversations, even when I was surrounded by a hundred nodding heads, I felt uneasy. It struck me as psychologically dysfunctional, no matter how noble the cause.

My doubts at the time traveled in two directions, however. Accompanying my unhappiness about the possibility that someone I cared about might burn himself to death was an intense curiosity about the sort of passion and commitment such an act would require. What brings a person to a point where he is willing to take his life on behalf of an idea? Was this the ultimate revolutionary action? It brought back memories of grammar school lessons in U.S. History, particularly when I had first heard of American Revolutionary Patrick Henry's plea to "Give me liberty or give me death." Indeed, it was only in the political realm that I had come across anything remotely similar to what I was wrestling with now. In so doing, my appreciation for how political Ananda Marga was grew significantly. Noticing the interface between politics and spirituality on this very personal level was a first for me at the time. Both seemed to fuel themselves on passionate belief, another cornerstone of ideological approaches I thought about more fully later.

In the period immediately after my departure, however, I was more focused on the psychological aspect of all this. I found myself comparing the magical thinking, the obedience to authority, and the "buzz" of excitement characterizing that early conversion stage with the way children behave in their younger years. This was the first time I had viewed conversion and its operation through the metaphor of an injured or needy child seeking something from a perceived powerful authority. It was the line in my earlier poem about a "the teary eyes of a lost and fearful child," written while undergoing therapy, that led me to considering this. What measure of "adultness" needs to be present in a person wishing to approach something with a truly open mind yet be able to do so without relinquishing sovereignty over his own affairs? Can a person be innocent and experienced at the same time?

It was a natural progression from questions such as these to questions about how Ananda Marga and other converting organizations related to vulnerability. What was the ethical grounding required of converting organizations towards those they were persuading and guiding? Were there *any* consideration of ethics when ideology was the primary motivating force for an organization?

There didn't appear to be. The psychological vulnerabilities of potential recruits to an ideology were either ignored completely or viewed as an open door for converting organizations to increase their numbers. Little stood in the way of doing this if the potential convert lacked the strength of identity to challenge or interrupt the process. Whatever state of strength that identity was in before getting involved, it came under additional pressure with the demand to move from an "old life" to a "new one," a demand every ideological organization makes. During this transition myself, I had been encouraged to open myself as wide as I could to the ideological foundations I was being exposed to, and upon which I was to build my new life. Although Ananda Marga encouraged openness in this regard, it had a limited understanding of, or interest in, the psychological gaps such openness exposed. By this I mean it fostered an atmosphere where people could acknowledge the shortcomings of society or of their former lives, but the psychological space such stories created was immediately back filled with ideological solutions. Dealing with one's old life was reduced to embracing the tenets of the ideology. This meant that any form of critical analysis or any process of open-ended exploration of one's past was not part of the culture. Irrefutable expert opinion on how to live replaced this much more difficult and complex task.

Neither Ananda Marga nor any other converting organization is equipped or interested in addressing psychological uncertainty. A person's old life is simply to be dropped. The only way vulnerability is viewed is as an opportunity to secure compliance from, and authority over, people. When I finally realized this fully, it transformed the naiveté I had carried into the organization as a 20 year old into the ethical anger of a 23 year old. That and similar moments contributed to the momentum that ultimately led to my departure from the organization.

Another thing that occurred in the aftermath of my involvement with Ananda Marga was that I began to appreciate how my conversion experience was far from unique. Yes, there were specifics to my story that were not universally shared, but the overall susceptibility that had led to my joining the organization ran deeply through society. I concluded this when I saw those around me struggling with similar issues, and in similar ways, as I was. I began to wonder if there was some sort of overarching psychological dynamic present in U.S. society that was fueling the incredible conversion rate to both eastern religious movements and to fundamentalist Christian groups. Sigmund Freud's notion that sexual repression was the primary cause of mental distress in late nineteenth century Europe, for instance, had fit logically and convincingly with the surrounding Victorian era culture's stringent emphasis on sexual restraint. Was there an overarching psychological dynamic of *this* time and place? If so, how did it influence people's susceptibility to conversion?

After I left the organization, I lifted my head and noticed more clearly the explosion of psychological and spiritual workshops, retreats, conferences and seminars that was occurring throughout California at this time. What were some of the shared motivations drawing people to these events? Waves of prominent therapists from existential, humanistic and later transpersonal schools of psychology were dropping in on places such as Esalen on the Big Sur coast to conduct workshops which included but were not limited to encounter groups, the ingestion of psychedelics, collective living experiments, the politicalization of psychotherapy, primal scream therapy, meditation, bodywork, and highly controlled conglomerate approaches to consciousness raising such as the Erhard Seminar Trainings (EST). Psychological and spiritual self-inquiry seemed to be occurring in every conceivable way: gently, confrontationally, in groups, individually, with clothes on and without them.

As the number of people engaged in all these explorations continued to grow, it seemed as though the willingness to participate had reached some sort of tipping point: *self-examination* was giving way, for many, to *self-absorption*. It had not only become acceptable to explore one's life, it had become something of an obsession to do so. Signs of unhealthy self-absorption were popping up everywhere on the workshop circuit: an inflated sense of self-importance, a retreat from the political sphere, and a growing sense of entitlement were all examples of this.

As the decade of the 80's began another broad, societal change became obvious. The focus of therapy was shifting from encouraging self-knowledge and expanding one's awareness to preparing an individual for *success* within mainstream society. A therapeutic landscape that had been dominated by existential-humanistic schools of thought was now embracing "middle ground" behaviorist strategies; therapies that still acknowledged the existence and importance of individual consciousness but placed the primary emphasis of therapy on behavioral change. Initial forays into this territory were through methods such as Albert Ellis' Rational Emotive Therapy, but newer, more sophisticated versions of this – including the whole range of clinical approaches that ultimately fell under the heading of Cognitive Behavioral Therapies – were sprouting up everywhere. These approaches focused much more intently on individual behavior, severing any linkage to the political awareness or spiritual concerns that had influenced a number of therapeutic modalities of the 70s. No longer was the idea of questioning the rationale behind how success was defined being questioned. No longer was its linkage to the ethics of the larger society part of the therapeutic landscape. No longer was its impact on politics a matter of concern. What mattered now was clearing up whatever psychological issues stood in the way of being successful in mainstream society.

During the 80s the dominant philosophy underpinning mainstream life in American society was shifting dramatically towards economic rationalism. Individual success was driving practically everyone, and had become synonymous with the accumulation of wealth. This approach is still firmly established in the minds, behaviors, and value systems of people today, 30 years later. At the time it was more embryonic in nature, seeming to reflect an energized rebirth of the materialism of the 50s. In the "restart" excitement of doing so, many in the 80s were quickly abandoning political causes, collective well being, and the pursuit of self-knowledge in favor of the pursuit of prosperity. It was a dramatic and noticeable shift, and it was being done wholeheartedly.

One notable dimension of this shift, however, seemed to be what *didn't* change. There appeared to be a thread linking the extreme experimentation of the 60s and 70s and the success-oriented strategies of the 80s. That thread was the self-absorption noted earlier. Self-absorption had woven a path through the countercultural experiments of the earlier period right into the heart of the economic rationalism of the 80s. It seemed to now be assuming the status of an accepted norm in contemporary society, impervious to the extreme fluctuations in the surrounding cultural orientation of that society. What did the staying power of self-absorption in these different periods of society, amongst people of very different political and cultural persuasions, indicate about the primary psychological dynamic of the times?

The cultural historian Christopher Lasch noted during the 70s that every age has its own particular form of pathology, which expresses, in exaggerated form, its underlying character structure[3]. What was the underlying character structure of this age? What had been normalized and integrated into day-to-day life? Was the greater social embrace of self-absorption a clue to this?

Society's tolerance level for every day self-absorptive behaviors seemed to be increasing on all fronts. Politicians who purposefully lied to their constituencies, for example, didn't appear to be held to account as fiercely in the 80s as they had been in the previous decade. Not only that, many of them were considered *strong* if they lied with a sense of conviction and certainty. This was in stark contrast to the example of Watergate, when this sort of behavior had been viewed as reprehensible, a flaw worthy of impeaching a president. Going back even further, deceitful behavior of this sort clearly undermined the values that had been embraced, however inconsistently, by social movements in the U.S. after WWII: the civil rights movement and the Vietnam War peace protests being the primary examples. It wasn't that deceitful, misleading behavior was anything new. It was that astonishment at it happening seemed to be deadening considerably. That astonishment was being replaced by two trends which had probably always been around but which were emerging with much greater force in the 80s.

The first was a powerless cynicism in the general population that ascribed unethical behavior as universally true of "everybody," and saw no way to do anything about it. This defeatist, passive attitude stood in sharp contrast to the social hopefulness that had characterized much of the 60s and 70s. It also stood *behind* the sunny appearances projected by everyone who had jumped aboard the wealth wagon, enticed by the seductions prosperity was promising. Those seductions were aimed at individuals, not at community improvement, and the ease with which wealth could be procured seemed to confirm the notion that social problems would simply solve themselves as the rising tide now in motion lifted all boats.

The second trend gaining traction at the time was a greater brazenness regarding Machiavellian power grabs, in politics but also more broadly. People engaged in such behavior seemed less concerned about covering it up and, in many cases, were viewed heroically not only by the media but by the overall population, particularly if their efforts produced financial success. Ethical problems were being viewed in a much less interested way. The more important consideration seemed to be whether ethical problems, in the context of an already stressful and overwhelming life, would directly and immediately affect an individual's own circumstances. Would anybody notice? If they did, would anything be done about it? The rising impunity with which politicians, corporate CEOs, religious leaders and others could now lie about issues without being held to account, issues which seemed to always involve some form of short term gain for a small, influential segment of the population, indicated that the answer to both these questions was increasingly "no."

The lack of any forceful objection to this trend was worrying. It highlighted the fact that what was deemed acceptable was being redefined, and in this process certain foundational values in the society were shifting. It could be argued that self-centered behavior had always been prevalent in American society, and that there was just as much, if not more, of it in earlier eras as there was in the 80s. Maybe so. The shift that was happening, however, was alarming not for its increased frequency but for its increased acceptance. It was a shift that not only tolerated but increasingly saw as *desirable* a trait which went far beyond mere self-absorption and which, in earlier eras, had been seen as dysfunctional. This trait fits easily into a society where the accrual of wealth and the pursuit of individualism are primary goals, and where the time and value placed on relationships, community, and service to others is considered subservient to these goals. This trait also cuts a wide swath through more serious mental complaints, often working in concert with them. It is a character trait whose momentum began in the 60s and which burst into full bloom in the 80s: *narcissism*.

A social fabric with a disproportionate emphasis on individualism, wealth, and excessive consumption had provided a fertile breeding ground for an explosion in and acceptance of societal narcissism. Narcissism is frequently seen as synonymous with self-absorption, but conflating the two is an oversimplification. It erases the significance of the other critical factors defining narcissism: *entitlement, acting without regard for personal boundaries, envy, magical thinking, arrogance, shamelessness and exploitation*[4]. These factors fill out the definition of a phenomenon that goes well beyond self-absorption, and make it easier to see how widespread, and tolerated, all these qualities have become.

These characteristics only become problematic when narcissism runs off the tracks, however. Developmental psychologists have always emphasized that successfully navigating through the narcissistic phase of growth as a young child is necessary if a healthy sense of confidence is to blossom later as an adult. Narcissism, in other words, is a *stage* of growth: a temporary phase of a young child's mental and emotional development, one requiring the skillful involvement of that child's caregivers if it's to be successfully negotiated. If it isn't it can, and often does, result in some form of narcissistic injury. The nature of that injury will be damage to a person's capacity to live his life in a way that accurately expresses his natural abilities; an inability to live a life that is in accord with aspirations he himself discovers. The extent of damage to this capacity varies from individual to individual.

Developing in a healthy way requires that the narcissistic stage of development be navigated in a way that results in the emergence of a solid personal identity; i.e. when a person's confidence ends up on stable but not inflated ground. Passing through narcissism successfully also means not getting stuck in looking to others for self-definition, because if that happens a person develops the habit of endlessly trying on identity rather than *discovering* it directly through a combination of exploration, reflection, and supportive feedback. Successfully navigating through narcissism teaches a person to stop short of the excesses characterizing narcissistic entrapment, particularly self-inflation, entitlement, and shamelessness.

As narcissism established its hold on U.S. society from the 60s to the 80s, most of the people writing about it did so because they saw fewer and fewer people passing through this stage in the healthy manner just described. Psychoanalytic theorists such as Otto Kernberg and Melanie Klein warned of the corruptibility of a narcissistically damaged personality, and its debilitating impact on a person's conscience. Journalist Tom Wolfe saw the rise of narcissism aligning with a third great religious revival in American society. Cultural historian

Christopher Lasch saw narcissism as a force that eroded society's sense of historical continuity – its increasing inability to do things in the present for posterity. Lasch also saw the increase in narcissistic behavior as an outgrowth of a growing resignation people had about the survival of society itself.

All this pointed to the fact that narcissism was becoming normalized in U.S. society. What did this mean? Firstly, it meant all the narcissistic character traits listed in the definition above would continue to increase. The implication of this was that narcissistic behavior would cease to be something people considered unusual. It would become tolerated, not because it was pleasant, but because it was everywhere.

A second implication was equally significant. When narcissism is normalized in a society, the value of discovering identity that healthy passage through this stage is meant to lead to diminishes. The motivation to do so disappears. It's replaced by an endless cycle of adopting identity from external sources. The result for anyone caught in such a cycle is that he never establishes a solid sense of self. The reason psychotherapists and developmental psychologists give for this cycle gaining traction in the first place is the failure of the care giving environment to allow a child the necessary freedom and emotional nourishment when he is young to experiment freely with his capacities within safe limits defined and provided by those caregivers. Devoting the time and energy to getting this balance right is a challenge most parents simply find too difficult. That difficulty leads them to direct their child to behave in ways that accommodate *their* expectations instead, setting up a huge obstacle to that child ever engaging directly in the process of self-discovery. This reflects not only the stresses those parents may be experiencing at the time but often their own unhealed narcissism, the fact that they may also have lived life out of a false sense of self and are now projecting their own unmet needs onto their children.

In a healthy environment where caregivers have solid identities and the capacity to love and nourish their children something else happens: parents allow their child to fully experiment with separating from them to try out his own ideas, but to also come back to them for emotional nourishment when his vulnerabilities and limitations come to the fore. They set appropriate limits without undermining the exploratory spirit. Through this "mirroring" process, the child grows up in a healthy environment, eventually gaining the necessary foundation for his real identity to emerge, solidify, and transform later as required.

The tricky part about all of this is that the public face of a person who has been narcissistically injured is that of a confident, self-assured person. The primary external difference between his experience and that of someone genuinely self-assured is that his persona has a strong element of *bluff* running through it. The bigger difference, however, is the interior experience of the narcissistically injured person. The confident image he has adopted masks the subterranean reality he experiences every day. That reality consists of ongoing feelings of low self-worth and a damaged capacity to feel a constructive level of shame when he has done something inappropriate to others. Those feelings have their genesis largely in the emotional abandonment he experienced from his caregivers. These are reinforced when the narcissist makes a decision that the only way to navigate a path to identity, and to acceptance from others, is to manufacture and live through a false self. This decision reinforces his initial sense of abandonment because, tragically, it signals the narcissistically injured person's abandonment of himself.

The behavioral result of all this later on is a life characterized by an ongoing and often desperate search for identity and individuality. Waiting in the wings for a person with narcissistic damage are individuals and organizations only too ready to provide him with that identity. False identities provided by predatory organizations are available in every direction, ready to secure the allegiance, money, and obedience of anyone still trying to sort out who he really is.

In the consumer world, this means convincing people that purchasing a product will fill the void that person feels inside. In the religious world, it means offering a way of life that promises an identity linked to enlightenment or salvation. These promises are "read" by a narcissistically injured person as opportunities to heal his wounds. Usually they are pursued intensely, fueled by an inflated view of self, and disconnected from any real identity. It is easy for such a person to believe that the right job, the right image, the right car, the right path are all that's needed for fulfillment, and that identity and role are equivalent. Roles adopted in this way are superficial in both the consumer world and the spiritual world, leaving the narcissistically wounded person scratching his head when he inevitably comes up against their limitations, wondering why the emptiness inside still remains.

Once I began to grasp how this cycle worked, I recognized that narcissistic injury had underpinned much of my own behavior leading up to and through my involvement with Ananda Marga. I found this recognition unsettling, but I couldn't turn from it. There was little comfort in observing that the same phenomenon appeared to be operating strongly in most of the population. Nobody seemed to think twice about people acting out low key, or not so low key, versions of narcissistic behavior in their organizations, in part because much of that behavior was now seen in a positive light. A person with narcissistic damage can be inspiring, charming, intellectually enticing, and wonderfully humorous: sometimes all within the space of 60 seconds. There is, of course, nothing dysfunctional about these qualities on their own. It's when those qualities mask more self-centered strategies that the situation can quickly turn pear-shaped. Clues that expose such strategies in every day life are often small, such as the many ways a person can surreptitiously manipulate others in his work or community environments out of envy. Or when a person withholds information from others in his organization knowing full well that it will damage them but advance his cause and, when it does, shows no remorse about that happening. Even when the clues are more obvious - people in positions of power invading the privacy of those working for them to the point of verbal or physical bullying, for instance - they are considered commonplace by most people. The response to those who point out such behaviors is usually one of ridicule and an admonition to either fight back in the same way or become more thick-skinned.

I grew alarmed when I realized that the role-hopping aspect of narcissism had been a major motivational factor in my decision to join Ananda Marga. Identifying myself as a seeker had put me squarely in the cross hairs of an organization offering the ultimate goal of enlightenment. If I didn't come to terms with my own narcissism and stayed enmeshed in this false identity, I was unlikely to be advancing towards greater self-knowledge anytime soon.

It was discouraging to look out more widely and see that the predominant societal means for engaging in narcissistic behavior had jumped from psychological and spiritual exploration to economic advancement, leaving untouched its steadily growing acceptance levels in society. The pursuit of success through adopting an identity that "aims to please" clearly formed as solid a foundation for the growth of narcissistic qualities as the previous era's focus on psychological and spiritual awareness eventually had done. Now that I had this awareness, I was confronted by the reality of having to deal with my own version of it. How would I do that? I didn't think my own narcissistic behavior had played out in an extreme fashion; nonetheless, it had definitely entangled my genuine desire for self-knowledge with a false identity, and had done so without my recognizing it for a considerable period of time. The question of disentangling these two threads from each other began to look both essential and difficult.

It was a short step to realize that in the world of ideological fidelity, where rigid adherence to the rules that promise identity and, in the case of fundamentalist versions, salvation, narcissistically injured people constitute the vast majority of participants. They are prime candidates for conversion. The well hidden needs of such a person surface when he senses, falsely, that an easy path to fulfilling those needs can be taken through adoption of an ideology. This makes him more susceptible to the emotional manipulations engineered by converting organizations to convince him he has at last discovered the truth about who he is and what his purpose in life is. The intensity of emotion that accompanies such a belief, the "born again" experiences he has, and the new found certainty which erases, temporarily, his lifelong habit of doubt can easily be funneled towards a fanatical and energetic promotion of whatever his beliefs become. Funneling such emotion into organizational obedience consolidates the conversion process. The content of the ideology doesn't matter. Cultural differences and doctrinal content take a back seat wherever narcissistic vulnerability exists, and the overlap between this vulnerability and susceptibility to conversion is extensive. Emotional conversions to causes of any sort reflect a narcissistically injured person seeking identity through a process of attachment to an appealing idea or person; a relentless pursuit of the mirroring process he never received growing up.

Clearly the genuine identity I had hoped to discover through my involvement with Ananda Marga had been derailed by the conversion process itself. The lure of the golden world, reinforced by narcissistic injury, had made it easy to compromise my own judgment, override my doubts, and allow myself to be converted. My insights about this came after I left, but even if they had occurred at the time, they would have been insufficient to pry me away from Ananda Marga. Not so long as I perceived I was gaining some sort of identity, however shallow and temporary that identity might ultimately prove to be. As noted earlier, my Ananda Marga identity felt absolutely terrific at the beginning of my involvement, deflecting any inclination I had to abandon it until it became abundantly clear something was out of kilter.

Understanding this began to partially answer a question I had about the link between psychological vulnerability and spiritual awareness. My vulnerability had exposed psychological flaws in my character, and it was now clear that the self-knowledge I sought was not going to be available to me until I first dealt with those flaws. An understanding of my personal psychology could not simply be sidestepped by my desire to access self-knowledge that confined itself to the content of a particular ideology. This was a first step in realizing that it takes considerable time, effort and support to recognize the pervasive influence of narcissism, and to learn to operate outside of its influence. I could see how easy it would be to continue to self-deceive and remain in false identities my entire life. Narcissistic inflation carries with it a kind of hyperventilated aliveness, enough to sustain not only one's self but others in a fantasy world that is superficially invigorating but ultimately devoid of authenticity.

The rapid increase of narcissism in society was also giving the lie to the assumption that people who had already passed through childhood would have less susceptibility to conversion simply because their maturity and critical faculties would have advanced to the point where reason and common sense would rule the day. All processes of persuasion depend on vulnerable receptivity, regardless of whether the person is a child or an adult, and regardless of whether that receptivity is a reflection of youth, psychological injury, or a genuine desire for self-knowledge. Vulnerability is woven through whatever sense of self a person possesses at a given point in time. Social scientists have for years demonstrated that life experience is no guarantee of the ability to resist being persuaded, influenced, or converted by other people later on in life. If identity is shaky, a person is susceptible to surrendering that identity to someone or some organization he perceives will be able to provide solidity for him. This is as easy to do as an adult as it is to a child in an early developmental stage.

It appeared as though society hadn't appreciated how susceptible each person is to conversion if he doesn't make the effort to discover identity rather than adopt it. An adopted identity provides too thin a foundation for a fulfilling life. Many people inherently recognize this, even if they don't always do so consciously. A person may be uncomfortably aware of the fact that his identity lacks a realistic understanding of his possibilities and limits. His conscience may point out that he secured his identity through a passive rather than active process. He may be perplexed by how the emotional exhilaration that first accompanied his sense of having "found himself" had vanished from the scene.

Unfortunately, people who have not had the experience of discovering identity directly will automatically turn to external sources to provide it to them repeatedly over the course of their lives. What else does a person know to do? This facilitates an organization's ability to prey on a fractured and underdeveloped sense of identity, and to profit by this damage. This holds true regardless of whether the predatory organization is spiritual or secular. Both count on the fact that people look to *consume* identity when they don't have experience discovering it for themselves. This external orientation, in combination with the thinness of identity that results, makes people susceptible to conversion for what could be their entire lives.

None of this means that a person can't heal narcissistic injury through the provision of love, security, the meaningful activities he is drawn to as an adult, and a commitment to work through problem areas in his life history in an aware and transformative way. Approaching the issue with a brave but humble heart will give him the opportunity to structure adult life and solidify identity in appropriate ways. A person's sense of identity is meant to strengthen and expand as he goes through life; it is meant to incorporate qualities such as a critical intellect and common sense. Healthy narcissism is not an oxymoron; it's the end result of a stage a person is meant to pass through in his early years. If it's not done then, it can be done later. From the platform of *real* identity that emerges from doing so, a person can subsequently discover values central to his life: values formed through the combination of experience, reflections about that experience, and the integrated feedback of other trusted and respected people he willfully takes on as his own. When identity is discovered and expanded in this manner, it serves its intended function of protecting a person from conversion to something radically different.

How common is it that people have this sort of solid identity? It's rare enough that ideologies continue to rope in converts willing to follow their dictates in large numbers. It's rare enough that most people in the U.S. define themselves primarily through their wealth, their possessions, and their career rather than through something that runs more deeply beneath these things. Ideologies fill the gap left in a person's development when he fails to recognize the importance of discovering his own identity because those around him during his childhood were either unable or unwilling to provide the containment and encouragement necessary for this to happen. How many families are capable of or motivated to provide the kind of healthy psychological environment a child needs growing up? As Lasch puts it,

> One of the gravest indictments of our society is precisely that it has made deep and lasting friendships, love affairs, and marriages so difficult to achieve. As social life becomes more and more warlike and barbaric, personal relations, which ostensibly provide relief from these conditions, take on the character of combat[5].

A child more often than not grows up in an environment where his needs may be partially met through the heroic efforts of dedicated parents, hardworking schools or devoted community members but, even when this is the case, those efforts can be undermined when the surrounding society is excessively tolerant of narcissistic behavior. In such an environment, the value of bringing people to adulthood whole rather than as stitched together pieces is pushed to the side. This greatly increases the likelihood that large numbers of children will enter adulthood with a strongly operational narcissistic character strategy or, more severely a full blown narcissistic injury. Securing one's identity is simultaneously a fragile thing and something that requires incredible courage. Its pursuit is something a person needs to persist in his entire life.

The fragility of this process is highlighted by the steady erosion of a psychologically healthy environment supported by the larger society; this is a foundation stone every person, family and community needs. This cannot be the case when society's focus is fixated on competitive self-interest. That attitude undermines the work many families do in loving their members regardless of their flaws, putting appropriate boundaries around a child's experience, and enabling him to discover his own identity through ultimately venturing out beyond those boundaries.

Converting organizations intuitively know this. They spend considerable time simulating a healthy environment through the creation of *surrogate families* designed to convince a person he can still have the family experience he missed. To people exposed to societally sanctioned narcissistic behavior every day or, more seriously, to anyone with narcissistic damage, a second opportunity to have such a family is irresistible.

In my desire to further understand the weave of psychological vulnerability and spiritual aspiration I had bundled together, I turned my attention back, once again, to my early days in Ananda Marga and the role the organization had assumed as my surrogate family during that time. Was what I had been offered too good to be true? Probably, but I needed to find out why.

---

3   Lasch, The Narcissist Society, p. 15
4   Hotchkiss, Chaps. 1-7
5   Lasch, ibid., p.10

Chapter 3

Surrogate Families

"Through the intermediary of the family, social patterns reproduce themselves in personality. Social arrangements live on in the individual, buried in the mind below the level of consciousness, even after they have become objectively undesirable and unnecessary—as many of our present arrangements are now widely acknowledged to have become."

- Christopher Lasch

"The demise of a sense of personal responsibility is the most significant consequence of submission to authority."

- Stanley Milgram

My first experience of the power of a surrogate family in an ideological organization came the summer after that initial talk on meditation, when I was invited to attend an Ananda Marga dharma chakra. I had been enjoying the meditation and yoga classes Ananda Marga offered at the Student Union, responding really well to new ways of calming anxiety and increasing self-awareness. That was enough to make me curious about how I could pursue things further. I decided to accept the invitation.

I had no idea what to expect on the night of my first dharma chakra. Shortly after arriving at the suburban home where it was held, I found myself sitting on the floor with about 15 other people, all of us receiving instructions about how the evening would progress. The first activity was to be the chanting of Sanskrit songs. That would continue until the guitar player or someone else in the group spontaneously began chanting the words *Baba Nam Kevalam*. This Sanskrit phrase apparently meant a lot of things. "Love is all there is," "The name of God is everywhere," and "Blessed is the world" were 3 of them. I remember thinking that the group might want to get a better translator, but I didn't say anything.

Once the Baba Nam Kevalam chant began, everybody was to stand up and begin doing *kirtaan,* or spiritual dancing. This consisted of swaying from one side to the other with both hands reaching up in the air, alternately dipping the big toe of one foot behind the other foot and then repeating the process to the other side. While we were doing this, we were to keep chanting and to "let your feelings take you towards a sense of unity with everything." This was to be assisted by dancing in front of this huge orange flag with various symbols on it.

I raised my head to look at the flag for the first time. I remember swallowing hard and making sure I contained the surprise on my face. There were four symbols on the flag.

The first was a downward pointing triangle. This, we were told, symbolized the meditation process: looking inward for self-knowledge. Because meditation on its own is insufficient for navigating through life, this triangle was intersected by the second symbol: an upward pointing triangle, signifying social service freely given in the world. Combined, the two triangles looked like a Star of David, at least from my western point of reference.

Just above the base of the upward pointing triangle, a centrally placed vertical line was said to represent "consciousness unbounded by anything." A horizontal line of the same length intersecting it formed a cross, and was said to be the "qualifying force" of consciousness: the moment where creation occurs and consciousness becomes self-consciousness. In other words, life becomes aware of itself through creation.

Attached to this cross were four smaller lines, their endpoints perpendicular to the endpoints of the four segments of the cross, all pointing in a clockwise direction. This transformed the image of the cross into that of a swastika.

I certainly wasn't the only one whose attention was riveted by this: a swastika sitting inside the Star of David. A brief glance around confirmed that not only was this symbol being stared at rather intensely, but people were having their own private, and strong, emotional reactions. I was no exception.

Of course this was explained as something quite different. The swastika was an ancient Hindu symbol representing the journey of consciousness back to its limitless state, the spiritual journey everyone must ultimately take. The clockwise direction of the swastika represented the rise of kundalini, the mysterious serpentine force resting at the base of the spine, waiting to be awakened so that it could, through meditation and other forms of spiritual practice, unwrap itself and begin its journey upwards through the chakras or energy centers of the body.

Ananda Marga ideology guaranteed the success of the spiritual journey to all who began it. No matter how many lifetimes it took, once a spiritual aspirant began to pursue Ananda Marga ideology, he would inevitably finish that journey. To symbolize this on the flag, the swastika had a half circle rising sun over the top of it, its end points touching down on the base of the outward pointing triangle. The final of the four symbols of what was called the *pratik*.

The primary association I had with a rising sun symbol was the Japanese flag. Combined with the swastika and the Star of David, I found myself envisioning World War 2 kamikaze pilots bearing down on the decks of U.S. aircraft carriers, and German stalags filled with Jews awaiting the gas chamber. It was not an easy symbol to dance in front of chanting "Love is all there is" without considerable cognitive dissonance.

But dance I did, along with everyone else, and I soon felt swept along by unexpectedly powerful feelings. Belonging, community, perhaps even the bliss spoken of by the word *ananda*. Worldly concerns evaporated as I gave my voice and feet free rein, intoxicated by this communal ritual. I felt myself transported; part of a community much larger than myself.

Afterwards, there was a spiritual reading followed by an evening ending shared meal. The elaborate vegetarian feast was certainly much more nourishing than the stuff

I'd been eating out of cans at my apartment, and the glow I felt continued to reverberate throughout the room. I left the evening walking on air, soaking up the emotional sense of belonging.

Never mind the swastika.

*   *   *

The night of this dharma chakra felt like a surprise birthday party, a kidnapping, and the birth of a first child all rolled into one. It pushed me so far into the territory of conversion that when I left Ananda Marga a few years later, I could only look back on that night in astonishment. The emotional surge of belonging somewhere had simply overwhelmed me. It had brought with it, unexpectedly, a level of anticipation that I had never had before.

Emotional intensity, however, comes and goes. As powerful as the night had been, I found myself the very next day noticing tiny voices of doubt inside my head. Voices whose origin lay in my memory, reminding me that my life hadn't just begun. Memory was trying to put context back into my life, reminding me of the 20 years I'd lived prior to this intense moment. What about the life I'd already built and the reasons why I had built it that way? Memory was the most potent force opposing the urge to cut ties with my old life and set off on an entirely different course.

It is, after all, no small thing to contemplate giving up a familiar existence without knowing where and how landfall will be reached on one's new journey, even when new levels of happiness have suddenly burst onto the landscape. The incongruities my memory threw in front of my awareness took sustenance from the alliance it formed with both my conscience and my reason. These three aspects of my awareness made every effort to ensure I kept their sensibilities on the radar screen. They generated challenging questions inside my head: *You're dancing in front of a swastika, Greg. Why aren't you more concerned? If you go further with this, who are you getting involved with?*

Questions such as these intensified the competition between what I had previously considered real and the possibilities I now saw in front of me. The battle ground for that competition was clearly going to be my identity. How solid was it? How enduring would the factors shaping it – the self-regard I had at that point, the influence of my family of origin, the impact of my culture and the institutions I'd grown up with – be in the face of an attractive but questionable alternative?

An ideological organization has to be seductive in its efforts to convert others. It has to minimize the impact of the reluctant parts of its potential convert's memory enough so that a person is willing to adopt its alternative reality. It does this by *shifting the focus* from the reasonable questions and doubts memory poses to the painful experiences it stores, then manipulating that pain to its advantage.

Ananda Marga understood, either knowingly or otherwise, that manipulating pain doesn't require digging up the past of its converts. It is far more effective to insistently, and exhaustively, promote an alternative reality. The emotional attractiveness of that reality, the elevating path if offers, provide a stark contrast to all the things that have gone wrong with a person's life previously. This is the best way to keep the swoon steadily moving forward. The organization achieves this through rituals that ensure everyone stays in an uplifted mood; it wants the waves of emotion it generates to last long enough for its conversion targets to travel past doubt into the safe, convincing territory of ideology. Once there, a new encyclopedia of reasonable ideas awaits. Once there, everything will make sense again, because it will all be explained: including, above all, why a person's "old life" is no longer relevant. Once there, a new identity can be adopted. All of this is possible only if the emotional attractiveness of a conversion swoon can be sustained.

The most effective way to do this is to create a surrogate family. Surrogate families are the external scaffolding used during the conversion process. They intensify the emotional sense of *belonging* a person without a solid identity desires. Belonging works socially in similar ways to how attachment works in the one-to-one relationship a young child forges with his immediate caregivers. It provides an additional layer of safety for a person to try out things, and a place to return to for sustenance after he has done so. Belonging provides a sense of security and love to a person.

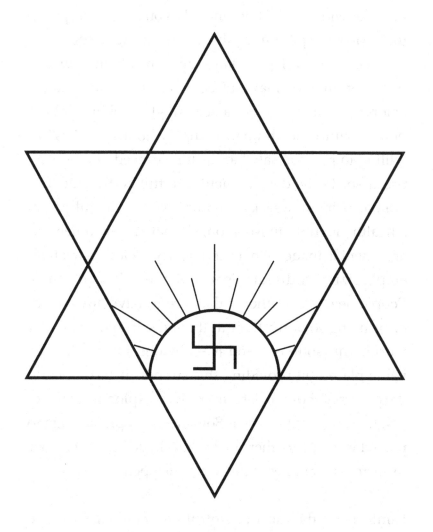

The Ananda Marga Pratik

If the initial bond with caregivers is not strongly formed, however – i.e. if narcissistic damage has occurred – the need for wider social bonding takes on a more desperate tone. Most people are capable of disguising desperation, but the need still percolates underneath the surface. A person may or may not be aware that the need for belonging functions like a searchlight seeking linkage points with other human beings whom it "reads" as willing to provide safe harbor for his need, a necessary precursor to the development of a full-bodied identity. Human beings are social in nature. No one can fully form a healthy identity in isolation, no matter how much this argument is made by hale and hearty societal narratives emphasizing individualism and the self-made man. People need each other if they are to have any chance of bringing forward their authentic self into the wider world. This sounds – and is – obvious, but the limited value placed on providing this support is testimony to the power of those societal narratives, explored at greater length in the next chapter. Somehow, people manage to push this need for others to the side. In doing so, the door to surrogate families is thrown wide open.

Families are the most powerful and familiar structure people associate with belonging. Everyone is impacted by the power of family, even if that impact comes from growing up without one. As awkward as the ritual of kirtaan in front of the pratik at my first Ananda Marga dharma chakra had been for me, I was willing to embrace it by the end of the night because I felt I was amongst a group of people who genuinely cared about me. It looked and felt like a welcoming family. In retrospect, coming to this conclusion about people I had just met was clearly unwarranted. How could I decide this so quickly? What prompted my willingness to put my old life to the side? The fact that these questions, in combination with my memory, couldn't diminish my leap into Ananda Marga was testimony to the power of its swoon, the narcissistic damage I carried, and the need for belonging woven into my psychological fabric. The ever-present fourth factor – my yearning for a return to the golden world – also blurred the landscape. These all intermingled on the night of that dharma chakra, and the labyrinth they threw down in front of me was one I had no way of successfully navigating at that time.

Emotive ritual is the key tipping agent in this process. The intoxication of a powerful ritual brings unconscious needs, fractured identity, and numinous aspirations all to the surface. A potential convert in the midst of being swept away may be encountering these forces for the first time in his life. It's not surprising in such circumstances that he is unable to make sense of what is happening.

Although my desire to reproduce some version of my mystical experience was well known to me at the time, neither my narcissistic damage nor my need for belonging was. I was aware in a general way that the latter existed but, as most people do when confronted by a painful history, I had simply gotten on with my life. I had convinced myself that I had dealt with the isolation I felt by pointing myself fully towards the future. Why be bothered with the messiness of events that could no longer be changed, wounds from the past, actions that could have been taken but weren't? Besides, it had become clear to me that the shortfalls of my family life, and of my parents in particular, were not a product of ill will so much as the combination of their own limitations and the fear they carried from their own distressing personal histories. I was eager to put that past to the side and move forward. I knew that human beings adapt exceptionally well to changed circumstances and are able to land on their feet despite, in some instances, severe trauma and repeated setbacks. Psychologically, this was the task I had set for myself.

What I was too ignorant to realize at the time was that doing this, while commendable in some respects, was also a form of denial. It prevented me from truly integrating important dimensions of my personal history. Once I left the organization I could attend to that history more mindfully through psychotherapy. During the period shortly after my first dharma chakra, however – and for two plus years more – the belief that I had found an identity and that I did belong somewhere were both reinforced by the emotionalized excitement driving my life. They combined to convince me that such work was unnecessary. Although doubt still persisted in faraway corners of my mind, I had concluded more strongly than at any other point in my life that I'd turned a corner that was permanent in nature.

What's missing from this equation is an understanding of how denial and a fractured identity join hands with surrogacy environments to create this shadow play. Denial plays its part by narrowing awareness of unpleasant emotions associated with difficult times. Its immediate goal is to keep the painful aspect of those events from overwhelming attention in the present. In doing so, it gives a person his ability to function, often quite competently. The cost of this narrowness, however, is the broader awareness a person needs to be able to notice that the adaptability denial has brought him requires him to operate on the surface of life, shielded from not just the deeper emotions he's protecting against but from a deeper experience of life itself.

Fractured identity and surrogacy play prominent roles in this scenario. The emotionalized excitement generated by powerful ritual overwhelms the defenses put forward by denial. This is especially true if the ritual is one where other people are present, confirming the ritual's validity through overwhelming, enthusiastic participation. The wave of emotion connected to a person's desire for identity, the wave of emotion attached to that person's desire for belonging, all come hurtling into the present when the ritual accomplishes its objective: breaking through a person's wall of denial and bringing all his unmet psychological needs to the surface.

Inside himself, the person is left swimming in a sea of those needs, now conscious but not necessarily identifiable to him. He'll feel all sorts of things, likely to include the following: relief from the psychic burden of keeping denial in place, exhilaration at being welcomed into something that looks like a family, and the beginnings of confidence associated with finding an identity.

Denial as a psychological tool is a blunt instrument, and it simply doesn't have the capacity to fend off a highly organized, structured assault on the barriers it has erected. Its Achilles heel in this regard is not just the external pressure trying to break it down, but the internal pressure a person feels to let his needs out of their box. That internal pressure gains tremendous momentum if it sees something in the outside world that looks like a safe landing place for those needs.

My denial had repressed the painful emotions associated with my psychological past enough so that, prior to that night, I was imagining my future in a positive light. I had already touched into a sense of liberation by virtue of leaving home for university. I knew I now had the opportunity to take charge of my life's direction. The atmosphere I was heading into in California in 1970 couldn't have been more ideal for pursuing this task.

This step of having now given myself the opportunity to push aside my denial and bring whatever unmet psychological needs I had to the surface was a positive one. Those needs, however, still remained in my unconscious. The concentrated power of the Ananda Marga dharma chakra prompted them to finally break through. Once that happened, I concluded this was the first of many steps that needed to be taken.

My eagerness to pursue those steps speaks to the effectiveness of surrogacy: to the hope it offers. Without any direct prompting on the part of anyone in Ananda Marga I decided, in addition to bringing these needs to the surface, I had to shed my larger, historical identity. It was, after all, in the "control room" of that identity that I had made the decision to use denial to keep the pressures of my unmet needs at bay. I associated that identity with the denial itself, and concluded that both stood in the way of the freedom I sought. This meant that despite having spent 20 years building that identity, I determined it simply hadn't taken me nearly as far into my life as the promise of what I saw unfolding before me on the night of the dharma chakra would do. Once I thought that, I simply tossed my old identity into the dustbin of history. It was an exhilarating, "born again" decision.

The next step felt natural and straightforward: adopt the identity Ananda Marga was offering me, and accept the belonging I was being offered by its larger community. This is a logical step to take when a person lives in a society where narcissism has been normalized and identity is sought in the external environment. When that environment includes not just a few people but a whole family of them cheering him on, it amplifies the psychological force bearing down on him many times over, making the decision to surrender an old identity much easier. It's difficult, in retrospect, to determine which aspect of the dharma chakra evening was more remarkable: the capacity of Ananda Marga's emotive ritual to pull me so forcefully into its orbit, or the inability of my old identity to stand its ground in the face of this effort.

In understanding this better, it's useful to deconstruct the elements that contribute to the creation of genuine identity. The attachment to a caregiver examined in the last chapter is the most powerful dimension of that process, but it's not the only one. In order for the genuine identity of a person to take root time is needed, particularly for a young person having his first go at it. Time for that young person's brain to develop. Time for relationships with family, friends, and community to deepen and strengthen. Time for self-awareness to blossom to a point where reflection is a trusted tool for the person, connected to an inner compass he trusts. Time to consider possibilities, and to test values in the world. If all these things settle into place, he accumulates the ballast to withstand concerted efforts of conversion when they don't match up with his own notions of self.

Surrogacy puts a person's strength of identity to the test through its deployment of two very powerful strategies. The first is to collapse the timeline normally associated with identity development. This is accomplished through the use of emotive ritual, whose success depends on three things: 1) The ability to shift a person's consciousness from its day to day reality to something exhilarating, 2) The use of a lot of people surrounding the person to reinforce the ritual, and 3) The use of art to directly impact a person's emotions.

Art in Ananda Marga rituals expressed itself primarily through dancing and singing. In a revival tent, it comes through the cadences of a ministerial sermon, or the laying on of hands, or talking in tongues. At a stage-managed corporate conference it happens through inspirational stories articulated about the company's CEO, sometimes backed by rock bands and light shows. It doesn't have to be good art, but it does have to be emotive. When emotions are aroused amongst a lot of people, it steers the gathering in the direction of passionately confirming that the life represented by ideological compliance is both possible and desirable. It makes it easier to take the plunge into deeper levels of commitment after that. Emotive ritual changes a person's consciousness by striking right at the heart of his unmet need for belonging, at any narcissistic wound he may have, and at any desire he may have to experience a numinous reality. It not only collapses the timeline for identity formation, it hands identity over to an organization so a person doesn't have to do the work of discovering it for himself.

> "A hell-fire faith that uses the theatrical techniques of revivalism in order to stimulate remorse and induce the crisis of sudden conversion; a savior cult that is for ever stirring up what St Bernard calls the amor carnalis or fleshy love of the Avatar and personal God; a ritualistic mystery-religion that generates high feelings of awe and reverence and aesthetic ecstasy by means of its sacraments and ceremonials, its music and its incense, its numinous darknesses and sacred lights - in its own special way, each one of these runs the risk of becoming a form of psychological idolatry, in which God is identified with the ego's affective attitude toward God and finally the emotion becomes an end in itself, to be eagerly sought after and worshipped, as the addicts of a drug spend life in the pursuit of their artificial paradise."[6]

The second strategy employed by surrogate families is *approximation*. People remember powerful emotions in general, not specific, ways. The smell of a dirty diaper found by a mother in her child's closet at home may approximate a battlefield odor she remembers from her days fighting in Iraq; that could be enough to trigger the emotions of fear or anxiety she had when she was there. Approximation is central in triggering incidences of Post Traumatic Stress Disorder, but a person needn't be this severely afflicted for approximation to have an impact. If his desire for belonging was not met in his family of origin, that desire doesn't just go away. The person imagines what it would be like to have this need fulfilled. Anything that comes close to an imaginary family – anything that might fulfill this need – will be enough to attract him. The desire for family I had in my own imagination certainly didn't include dancing in front of a swastika embedded in the Star of David. That didn't matter, because once the ritual was in full swing, the feelings that were evoked matched my imagination very closely.

Converting organizations understand that the best way to approximate a person's familial hunger is to get that person to spend increasing amounts of time with other organizational members. This was not a stated objective in Ananda Marga; it didn't need to be. If a person is suddenly doing everything of consequence with new people who appear to sincerely care about him, this is close enough to evoke idealized notions of the family life he never had. The important factor is to approximate a person's internal notion of an idealized family enough that he is drawn further into the organization's orbit.

I entered the Ananda Marga orbit quickly because of a completely unplanned event that illustrates this phenomenon well. An Ananda Marga member I had met at that first dharma chakra turned up at my apartment a week or two later and asked if he could live with me. It is not particularly unusual for college-aged youth to seek living arrangements with people they don't know particularly well yet. I liked this person and it was easy to say yes to his request.

What I hadn't factored into my decision was his commitment to Ananda Marga. Once I opened the door to his becoming my roommate, my life turned upside down overnight. In only a matter of days I found my walls covered with moral codes and posters of meditating monks. My bookshelves swelled with books written by the guru. A puja (worship) table to meditate in front of appeared in the living room. A vegetarian diet was now the order of the day in the household. I quickly and willingly embraced the daily rituals of this more experienced Ananda Marga member into my life.

Members ambitious in their desire to follow an organization's precepts are the most potent emissaries of that organizations' ideology, even if they aren't intentionally dispatched for such a purpose. It was effective in my case not just because I liked my new roommate, but because he was part of a larger world into which I had already stepped. This world approximated the trappings of family I desired closely enough to assuage the lack of it in my childhood; it promised resolution to troubled aspects of my history.

Manipulating memory through techniques such as collapsing developmental timelines and approximation has become a high art in our age of persuasion. Success in that endeavor has become easier because the more a one-dimensional emphasis is placed on individualism, the greater the unconscious desire to belong to a community becomes. This paves the way for the effectiveness of surrogacy techniques. The desire for community makes a person vulnerable; it also makes him a target of converting organizations devising ways to take advantage of that vulnerability. Both these techniques are most effective when unconscious needs for belonging are no longer being denied. Once that happens, a person looks to fulfill his needs in present circumstances.

Psychotherapy has known about this for ages, at least since Freud. It was Freud who gave a name to one particularly common expression of this phenomenon: transference. Transference is when a person redirects emotions felt in the past about someone towards a person in the present. Freud saw everyone as susceptible to the "biological time machine" of transference, capable at any time of transferring past emotions, based on unmet psychological needs, into the present.

If an environment is perceived as safe, this is more likely than not to happen. A person who has not previously experienced a reliably safe environment before will, over time, find cracks in his walls of denial and seek fulfillment of his psychological need from others in the present. Most schools of psychotherapy concur that people do this instinctively, as a means of giving themselves another opportunity to understand and work through issues that have not been resolved at an earlier stage of development. The duty of a psychotherapist in this context is to respect but not believe in the transference put forward by the client: to see it for the imaginary relationship it is. The most common example of this is the client emotionally neglected as a child who sees a therapist as an adult and finds the attention he receives approximates what he imagined he should have experienced from his parents growing up. This alone is enough for transference to be activated. The client will unconsciously act, in small and large ways, as if the therapist can give him some version of the bonding his parents failed to give him. Transference can play out through something seemingly as small as getting angry at the therapist if the perceived love he is getting needs to stop because the therapy session time has expired. The therapist's job is to not, in turn, become inflated or deflated by these attentions but to instead allow the transference to occur, and then work with a free part of the client's adult attention to expose it for what it is: emotions from the past breaking through to the present and distorting present realities and relationships.

When a therapist treats a client's transference as something real, however, he engages in the same magical thinking as his client. Through this counter transference he becomes inflated with the role the client has assigned him, and in doing so may cross appropriate professional boundaries. This can be at a minor level, such as accepting gifts from a client. At a much more serious level, it could lead to a therapist having sexual relations with the client. It is the exception, not the rule, for a therapist to engage in counter transference with a client. The professional training and the supervision he gets from other clinicians serves as a firewall against this possibility. It does still happen on occasion, however. The fact that it does despite all the safeguards, oversight and training built into the profession indicates what powerful, compelling forces transference and counter transference are. It also demonstrates the perils inherent in any surrogacy environment.

The authority figure in a surrogate family is under no professional constraints when he faces the unmet psychological needs of his potential converts. There has been no training in handling transference, no code of ethics to hold him to account, and no overview of his actions by a psychologically skilled supervisor. He is, on the contrary, expected to be persuasive and to "make the sale" for his organization. When people transfer unmet psychological needs onto him during the conversion process, the authority figure will accept it eagerly for one simple reason: it gives him additional powers of persuasion over the convert. For example, a religious convert who believes he has been born again because of the guidance of a Christian minister may find himself viewing that minister in a fatherly light. If that minister does nothing about this misperception – or worse, if he encourages it – the unconscious transference to him will grow. If the minister misperceives this affection as something real in the present rather than the expression of an unmet need from the past, his counter transference also grows. All of this increases the power he has to influence this convert in very serious matters, including but not limited to his commitment to the minister's ideology, how he conducts his sexual life, or how he manages his finances. If the minister is particularly predatory, sexual abuse is likely to be the main way the transference-counter transference scenario plays out. The dramatic increase in the number of major churches whose authorities have engaged in sexual abuse of members of congregations in their care, often but not always children, is largely attributable to a failure of untrained religious authorities to deal professionally with the issue of transference. The psychotherapy profession actively recognizes that people are social beings craving belonging and the most important people surrounding a person shape that identity hugely: his family, or a substitute for his family. The strength of a person's desire for belonging will prompt him to trust others to a very deep level if he considers that person and the surrounding environment safe enough to do so. This trust, the strength of his need, and the porousness of his identity all make him highly susceptible to being captured by his own transferential reactions. The need for this to be recognized and respected by those who are privileged to witness it is paramount. When people are ideologically motivated, however, they are more likely to manipulate this need than they are to respect it.

Surrogate families set the stage for this manipulation by providing the environmental triggers necessary to entice transferential reactions out of the woodwork: emotive ritual, continuous exposure to large numbers of like-minded people, and regular articulations of ideological reasoning explaining it all. These all serve to stimulate desires carried in the imagination of the convert, and to generate repeated opportunities for transference-counter-transference issues to emerge. When they do, ideological agents of conversion are at the ready to steer a person's vulnerability more deeply towards allegiance to their organization. The greater the frequency with which approximation is applied, the higher the success rate of conversion.

At the time of the dharma chakra, my internal decision to deepen my commitment felt like nothing more than taking a next step: a no brainer that would bring me new levels of fulfillment. It was easy to take on the identity being provided externally. What I couldn't do at the time was hold fast amidst the powerful emotions of need, navigate through them in a way that led to some kind of genuine self-knowledge, and then construct identity based on that self-knowledge. It was not just that it was easier to adopt the ready-made identity being put in front of me – it was also incredibly uplifting to do so.

The process of adopting identity from an external source needn't have all the drama that the story I've described here has. It happens in more low-key ways every day; its commonality, in fact, means that it goes almost entirely unnoticed in society. When an employee in a financial advisory firm that's running a Ponzi scheme deliberately alters records to fool a regulatory agency, he's adopted an ideological identity that aligns him with the idea that pursuing wealth at all costs is what matters. When a model takes drugs harmful to her health, she buys into an adopted identity supporting an ideology that beauty takes precedence over her own health. Both people in these examples may tell themselves they're doing what they're doing to stay employed, which may also be true. It doesn't change the erosion of values the person may believe he holds, and the steady redirecting of how he sees himself to align with what some external source says it should be.

The invisibility of adopting identity is reinforced further by the fact that a person who does so not only looks normal, he often looks exemplary. He can forge a dynamic career path, accumulate extraordinary wealth, and manifest all the other outward signs of success society values. If he does so in the face of a difficult psychological history, his achievements are considered all the more remarkable. This is one of the benchmarks contemporary society uses to define a successful life. Whenever a person overcomes long odds in his external struggles to achieve something no one thought possible, his example is held up as a model for all to follow.

The problem with society's applause of external transformation is that the question of whether a person has done the same thing inside himself is put to the side. Fullness of being, including the capacity to act on the gifts and talents a person has to contribute in the world, requires walking a fine line between getting on with things despite obstacles and ensuring that doing so isn't a way of avoiding an inner transformation that needs to happen. External adaptation can look inspiring when it demonstrates determination, courage and creativity irrespective of the setbacks a person has suffered. Sometimes, however, these qualities aren't as profound as they look. For some people, starting a company that achieves worldwide success may require considerably less courage than devoting the necessary time required to be a trustworthy and committed friend. Another person might find securing an Olympic gold medal to be a cakewalk compared to extending the compassion required of him to assist a dying parent in the latter stages of life. The remarkableness of any external change ultimately depends on what level of transformation occurs inside the person. If someone has overcome enormous external obstacles but experiences no lifting of his inner anxiety, no easing of his self-absorption, no calming of his private fears, then what have his accomplishments brought him? Have they connected him to a clearer sense of who he is? Have they given him an appreciation for how much his success hinges on factors beyond himself? Is he more aware of the responsibilities that success demand of him, including the responsibility of contributing something to the wider world?

It's always assumed that dramatic story lines signify internal shifts, but this assumption is faulty if questions such as these cannot be answered affirmatively. It's certainly true that an increase in self-knowledge can, and often does, accompany dramatic external shifts. It's also true, however, that the external shifts that meet with society's approval can prompt someone to be more aggressive, more greedy, or more superficial. If an increase in self-awareness has not accompanied external success, and if unconscious psychological needs are still invisible to the person, he is vulnerable to taking on the alternative realities provided by surrogacy. Surrogacy will speak to an unconscious desire to address those needs. Wholeheartedly adopting Ananda Marga's ideology was, for me, an external task easier than the inner transformation I needed to do: coming to terms with the reality of my mother's abandonment of me, and the subsequent lack of a family that was capable of showing me I belonged in the world. I climbed the ladder of Ananda Marga's hierarchy all the way to a position at its world headquarters in a relatively short period of time. Compared to the therapeutic work I later did on my psychological issues, that was easy.

Another way of saying this is that external circumstances are meant to be a catalyst for the pursuit of self-knowledge: a way of prompting a person to rise to a challenge and become a better human being in the process. The definition of "better" is not for anyone else to determine for that person. If a deeper awareness has been achieved, the person will know this inside himself. That knowing is what counts; it's what strengthens a person's inner compass. If his inner compass becomes something he trusts, he will rely on it when challenged to expand his identity yet again in the future. Fame, wealth, and other external trappings of success are the wrong measures to use in determining if a person has genuinely done something to increase his self-knowledge, because these rely solely on the surrounding society's narratives for their definition. The hard work of inner transformation, when it's achieved by the person, is what leads him to discover rather than adopt identity in the future. It is what plugs him into an aliveness based on awareness rather than emotionalized excitement.

As straightforward as doing this may sound, the reality of how it unfolds is often frustratingly convoluted. The role of surrogacy for me was anything but clear-cut, as I found out during these early years in Ananda Marga. My psychological needs at the time of attending my first dharma chakra as a 21 year old were mostly hidden from me. This was partly a function of youth, and partly a function of the emotionality of my personal history. It was also, however, a function of the influence of the surrounding culture, and of random events that thrust themselves into the landscape of my life at unpredictable moments. Such factors combine in ways unique to every individual, which is why no ideology, no matter how appealing its ideas may be, can make any claims on an ultimate truth. Particularly on the external pathways a person must supposedly follow to find it. For some people, that pathway may involve religious devotion. For others, it may mean getting a job as a truck driver. What matters are not the external factors, but whether a person can reliably trust his own inner compass. If he can, it's a sign he has done the work of discovering identity rather than adopting it. That work requires flexibility, open-mindedness, and a non-dogmatic attitude: all factors running in opposition to the organizational commitment, single-mindedness and compliance demanded by ideological approaches.

This doesn't mean organizations can't support a person pursuing self-knowledge. If an organization is sincere in its desire to address the psychological needs of its members, and to deal with them in a way that is respectful, it must first alert itself to some foundational principles the psychotherapy profession has known about for some time: 1) Psychological needs reside in a person's unconscious mind, and it's quite possible to avoid *ever* examining them. These needs are shaped mostly by a person's history, his environment, and his genetics but, irrespective of their source, even getting them to surface is hard work and avoided by the vast majority of people. 2) The needs of the psyche are not the only thing in the unconscious. That's also where a person's aspirations, gifts, and the seeds of his creative engagement with the world sit, waiting to awaken. 3) There is no firewall between needs, aspirations, traumatic memories, special talents, and any of the other contents of the unconscious. They circulate freely amongst each other, and, even if a person is successful in shining a light on any of them, his capacity for mistaking one for the other is almost infinite. He may think he is pursuing an aspiration when he is really fulfilling a need. He may interpret a spiritual impulse in personal psychological terms. 4) The decision an individual makes to discover rather than adopt identity unlocks the greatest potential he has for accelerating ethical development, for expanding his awareness of others, and for positively shaping overall character. It nudges that person towards forming a healthy relationship with his unconscious in ways that, if done skillfully, allow him to gain various levels of mastery over forces previously hidden to him.

When a person chooses not to discover identity, his needs and aspirations still seek outlets for expression. They just do so in distorted ways. They bang against the density of his life, trying to break through into his awareness, at whatever level the person is capable of understanding. This process is amplified by the fact that everyone not severely damaged or in some special genetic category wants some sense of aliveness to characterize his existence, even if he doesn't know that he wants this. If he pursues aliveness through adopting identity, it shifts his focus to the benchmarks associated with external success. These fail to ever bring him lasting satisfaction; people are built for more than this. In the process of turning a blind eye to self-discovered identity, it also means a person's life will be punctured every now and again by a feeling of existential hollowness. Most people learn to repress that feeling through the infinite variety of psychologically dysfunctional strategies available to all of us to do so.

None of this is news to anyone who seriously pursues a self-aware life. All of it, however, is generally ignored by organizational efforts that promise to fulfill a person's unmet needs but haven't the ability or intention to do so. Testing the sincerity of an organization's intentions requires asking the question: "If the organization provides an environment where a person can learn ways to access and trust his inner compass, is that organization willing to genuinely support, rather than manipulate, that person when his unmet psychological needs emerge in the process?" Ideological organizations are incapable of making such a guarantee, because their conversion objectives dominate every action they take.

As a result, manipulation of psychological need becomes commonplace in ideological environments, and surrogate families are one of the biggest weapons in the their arsenal for achieving this. After my initial Ananda Marga dharma chakra, my need to belong was strong enough that warm good will, attentive listening, and a like-minded community was seduction enough to convince me to take the next steps of engagement. Riding alongside those psychological needs was my genuine aspiration for self-knowledge. The emotionality attached to all this, the way the different factors interlocked with each other, overtook my capacity to critically analyze the intent of the Ananda Margiis trying to persuade me. I saw myself as being assisted, not converted.

This raises a huge question of the relationship of surrogacy to ethics. Religious groups, marketing agencies, governments, military groups and other organizations intent on converting others to their cause or product have wide ranging levels of understanding about the psychological needs of their potential converts. Manipulating vulnerability to turn those needs to their advantage can be accidental; sometimes, it's even unconscious. I never knew for sure as a 21 year old how much psychological understanding was behind Ananda Marga's use of rituals such as dharma chakras, private interviews with monks, and inspiration-based retreats. Clearly, all of these things were intended to convert people and gain greater levels of commitment to the organization's ideology. They were overseen by authorities who, to all outward appearances, were sincere in the belief that their ideological teachings were the best way to change the world in a positive manner. Their intentions did not seem to be consciously predatory.

Does innocence of intention, and the lack of psychological understanding it reflects, excuse an organization bent on persuading others from ethical responsibility for the consequences of its actions? How does it compare to more consciously predatory organizations – some of the marketing firms employed by large corporations, for example – who deliberately seek ways to manipulate vulnerability to create greater profit or advantage?

While an argument for a qualitative difference between these two examples can be made, they nonetheless share in common the fact that the persuasion efforts they make are conscious. Those efforts proceed regardless of the depth of understanding about the psychology operating beneath the surface and, in the end, that ignorance is no excuse for an organization's lack of self-reflection. Every organization is ethically responsible for the actions it takes to persuade people over to its cause. What organizations do to persuade people outside their boundaries is one of the most critical, and ignored, ethical dilemmas of our times. Nonetheless, most organizations excuse themselves from taking responsibility for the impact of their persuasive efforts by saying that their targets possess the free will to make their own decisions. They do indeed.

Freedom of choice does not, however, mean that the intention behind bending a person's free will in the "right" direction should go unquestioned. Constructing surrogate families and other shadow realities to secure ideological commitment is only considered fair game when the background narratives of a society place self-interest individual initiative, and competitive advantage ahead of the psychological well being of the larger community. Most organizations that employ surrogacy strategies know that free will unattached to a solid identity is capable of pushing a person's decisions into the realm of regressive fantasy. When the background values emphasized by the larger society revolve around self-interest this crucial piece of knowledge represents an opportunity, not a caution. Persuading others to adopt an ideology, even against that person's will, takes precedence over any other concerns. What price does society pay when it allows an organization to be free to persuade others but fails to hold them to account for their actions? What responsibility do the individuals who engage in this behavior on behalf of their organization have?

Surrogate families heighten the ethical issue of persuading a person against his will through their *intentionality*. That intentionality leads to an amplified psychological force focused on accomplishing the organization's goals. Their attacks work in the short run because life gets better when it funnels itself through focused, unshakeable beliefs shared with others. Shared belief with others is a powerful simulation of society's most revered social structure: the family.

Feeling better inside one's self, however, does not absolve a person of his wider personal responsibilities, including his ethical responsibilities to a broader community. The critiques of narcissistic self-absorption written in the late 70s and early 80s made this point repeatedly. Where had political awareness gone? Did the push for improving one's self associated with that era actually reflect a pessimism people had about affecting anything more than that? Did that sense of pessimism run even deeper, into fatalism about humanity's future, steering more and more people in the direction of navel gazing?

These are huge questions, all of which have an enormous bearing on the issue of personal responsibility. Where and how does this fit in? Were all the new activities I engaged in with Ananda Marga – some of which required boldness, and all of which were increasing my confidence – a sign of a willingness to take on increasing responsibility? It seemed so in the excitement of those early days. I took on everything the organization asked of me. That certainly made me reliable. It also made me more productive. How much do reliability and productivity reflect responsibility? How much do they reflect something else?

Responsibility in the broadest sense of the word implies a commitment to act according to what a person "knows is right." How does he make that determination? If he doesn't have a strong inner compass, he'll have limited capacity to do so. He'll depend instead on the social structures put forward by the ideologies he has adopted as his own. Direct perception about what is right, what is the responsible thing to do, will be filtered through a web of ideas he has acquired. I realized when I looked back on my experience in Ananda Marga that my perceptions, and knowing how to act in a responsible manner, were increasingly confounded by the efforts I was continuously making to interpret the environment around me in ideological terms. I allowed the world to directly affect me less and less, because I attributed the positive changes in my life to the discipline of filtering it through Ananda Marga's perspective. Responsibility for my own inner compass was steadily set to the side, replaced by compliance to a well-articulated body of ideas. In the beginning stages of my involvement with Ananda Marga, when those ideas excited me, and when the surrogate family surrounding me seemed to be satisfying my unmet psychological needs, this was not problematic. The question never arose because the ideological filter I was imposing on my direct perception provided me with a sense of belonging and an opportunity to focus my energy on intellectually appealing ideas.

As time went on, however, more direct experiences contradicted Ananda Marga's ideas about the world and fought their way through the swoon I was in. It was then that I recognized that my deepest responsibility was to my own awareness. That awareness clearly could be fooled when it filtered experience through ideology. The challenge of acting responsibly was to keep awareness foreground enough, unimpeded by ideology, to join with the courage responsible action demands. It meant being fully present in a situation, so that ideas can be challenged when they don't match direct experience. Being fully present goes hand-in-hand with a person taking responsibility for discovering rather than adopting his identity. Navigating successfully through the identity discovery process demands presence of mind; it requires a person to summon up whatever reservoirs of courage he possesses and to act responsibly, in line with his own perceptions.

Surrogate families manipulate the issue of responsibility very adroitly. Once a person has taken on an adopted identity, he will be asked to do things in the world that reinforce that identity, i.e. to equate personal responsibility with compliance to the organization's ideology. Once he begins doing this, it becomes progressively easier for him to absolve himself of responsibility to any wider community. He views anyone outside of the ideology as "other." His adopted identity conforms further each time he does this: and his capacity to act ethically in the world weakens.

Most people consider themselves immune to this sort of influence because they aren't part of an "extreme" group. The behavior such groups engage in through activities such as born again rituals, surrogate families, and stridently political efforts to do whatever it takes to steer society in the direction they want it to go all look foreign, and irrelevant. Because of this, most people wrongly consider themselves immune to the ways their own needs for belonging can make them susceptible to handing over their sovereignty, and the authorship of their identity, to a powerful authority. The naiveté of this perceived immunity was the point psychological researcher Stanley Milgram bluntly made in his astounding experiment in 1963.[7]

Milgram thought people would be very capable of resisting the influence of authority when he carried out his famous experiment that year. He wanted to demonstrate that the obedience of the German population to the fascist ideology of Adolph Hitler in WWII was an anomaly, something that wouldn't repeat itself in the United States. So under the guise of a "learning experiment," he put an ad in the newspaper requesting volunteers to participate in his research in exchange for a small fee for their time. His sample population turned out to represent a wide socioeconomic range of the surrounding community.

Each volunteer was paired with a confederate of Milgram's, a person whom the volunteer thought was just another volunteer like themselves but who secretly had a specific role to play in manipulating the experiment at crucial points. These confederates were paired with a genuine volunteer, and in all instances the confederate was designated the role of learner and the volunteer that of teacher. Both were then taken into a room where the learner would sit and be shown an electrical device that would lightly shock him or her for wrong answers. To convince volunteers that this would genuinely occur, each of them was given a sample shock of 5 volts.

The learner then remained in the room while the teacher went to the other side of the wall from where the learner sat and read off a word pairing list through a microphone system. The learner had to memorize the pairs so that when the teacher said the first word of the pair a second time, the learner was expected to say the second word. If he didn't, he would receive a shock.

Furthermore, each time the learner got an answer wrong, the shock level was to be increased by the teacher. In front of the volunteer teacher was a shock generator, indicating increasing voltage and leading into areas clearly marked with warnings such as "extreme intensity," "danger," and "XXX." Next to the volunteer teacher was the experimenter in a white coat with a clipboard. If the volunteer ever showed any hesitancy in continuing to shock the learner, the experimenter would say things such as "The experiment requires that you continue" or "You have no other choice, you must go on." No other coercion other than these statements was used by the experimenter towards the volunteers.

Since the confederate in the role of learner was not really trying to learn anything, he would deliberately get answers wrong to see if the real volunteer would continue to increase the level of shock he was administering. Milgram predicted that the majority of people would stop early in the process, when the learner started to express pain at the shocks. He even had the confederate say things that indicated his health was at risk at various points along the voltage scale, such as "I have a bad heart" or, towards the end of the scale, screaming. Despite this, 64% of the experimental subjects shocked the confederate to the maximum level. 95% went beyond the 50 volts where Milgram thought the vast majority would stop. At about 80% of the way up, after the confederates had expressed concern about their health, had screamed and protested, they stopped answering altogether. In their complete silence, 64% of volunteers continued to shock learners to the end of the scale, 450 perceived volts.

Of course, the confederate did not receive any actual shocks, and the volunteers received debriefing and counseling after participation. The astounding obedience exhibited by Milgram's subjects, however, was repeated in later experiments[8] and points to a persuasion continuum everyone is on. A person's point on that continuum is not static; it changes in accordance with a number of factors. The important point at the moment is that a person's location on that continuum determines whether the persuasive intentions of converting organizations through various forms of surrogacy will be successful.

As already noted, people resist the notion of seeing themselves as susceptible to conversion and blind obedience because they associate it with extremism. This fails to acknowledge the machinery of influence deliberately employed everyday in politics, government, religion and business. It fails to acknowledge the thinness of identity. It fails to acknowledge the strength of everyone's unconscious need for belonging. Denying the possibility of acting in extreme ways, in other words, blinds a person to seeing the forces that lead to excess. To the British government in the eighteenth century, the idea that American colonists would see their rule as anything other than benevolent was perplexing. When confronted with the likes of Patrick Henry announcing he would take death over a life without liberty, it would have seemed too extreme, too unhinged, to take seriously. In the context of the self-perception carried by the vast majority of British society, it was. In the context of a budding American independence movement, however, such words epitomized the very definition of sanity and courage. To recognize this would have required the British to step outside of their own ideological perspective and into the ideological perspective of their subjects.

The brilliance of Milgram's experiment is how clearly it demonstrates the gradual path to extreme behavior. There was nothing outlandish in the appearance of Stanley Milgram's experimental assistants, dressed in the conventional laboratory coats of the times. These assistants did not use any physical coercion. They simply said things such as "The experiment must continue." When people gradually and willingly acquiesce to authority, they end up performing abominable acts of obedience later looked back on with regret. Ethical boards prohibit experiments such as Milgrams' to take place today. If a contemporary version of this were allowed, would the results be any different? It's highly unlikely they would be, but rest assured: the belief people have that they would act differently would probably be greater than 90%!

A person's blindness to conversion susceptibility is almost total, and it increases when he is exposed to effective forms of surrogacy. He fails to make connections between what happens to others and the persuasion and influence barrage he submits to on a daily basis. That barrage invariably appeals to a person's desire for belonging. By shrugging off his compliance to external agents intent on bending his will to their objectives, he ignores his own vulnerabilities. He fails to recognize that when he is confronted with authority figures who are not exotic, who represent the very mainstream of the society in which we live, who are dressed just as he would dress if he were to be employed in the same position, and whom he trusts, he falls into line very quickly.

Revisiting Milgram's experiment made me wonder how my own susceptibility to conversion had been influenced by my mystical experience. Wouldn't the fact that this experience had lifted me completely out of all of society's trances have served as a caution about persuasive manipulations? Wouldn't my knowledge of a broader reality have protected me from more mundane influences in some fashion?

The fact that I had directly experienced an altered state of consciousness so much more powerful than anything I'd ever known didn't protect me in the least from my psychological need for belonging. The desire for security and love underpinning belonging circulates in the unconscious side by side with aspirations, gifts and the desire for self-knowledge. They are woven together, and frequently confused with each other. Experiencing a moment some people would describe as "enlightened" didn't override the push inside me for those needs to be satisfied. The urgency of psychological needs, their ability to blind perception, is not to be underestimated. When no solid identity exists to put them into perspective, when no effort to unlock denial and pursue self-knowledge is made, that urgency will scratch and claw its way into behavior. It will find ways through the strongest denial, even if it that means affecting the physical health of a person. It will interpret the external world through the lens of its own desperate appetite.

My experience with Ananda Marga's surrogate family efforts revealed how powerfully surrogacy influences identity formation. The foundation for the success of a converting organization's contextual manipulation is put in place psychologically before a potential convert even arrives on the scene: through his lack of a solid identity. The habit of adopting identity has its origins in a person's unsupported navigation through the narcissistic phase of childhood development. The shadow realities of surrogacy prey on adopted identity by throwing up a structure that approximates something a person has missed out on and still desires. In this way, surrogate families take ideological commitment to the next level. The realities they represent needn't be exact, they needn't be continuous, and they needn't be intellectually airtight. Getting people to mistake a shadow for the thing it represents is primarily a function of tightly structuring the environment, manipulating the psychological need stored in a person's painful memories, and either disallowing or short-circuiting any activities that might lead a person down a path of self-discovery.

Does this mean that surrogacy itself is without merit? That depends on an individual's awareness of the underlying values he is either adhering to or compromising when he embraces a surrogacy environment. Consider an increasingly common example in contemporary society. If a couple wants to have a child but is unable to produce one themselves, one option available in some western countries is for that couple to provide their genetic material to inseminate a surrogate mother in a third world country. A surrogate mother in India earns on average $7500 dollars for this task. This is enough, if she's from a rural area, to survive on for 15 years. The parents paying for the service also save money: all the savings associated with not having to become pregnant themselves. Assuming the arrangement is not coercive, such a scenario nonetheless requires a significant values-based decision.[9] By treating pregnancy, the surrogate mother, and babies primarily as economic commodities, considerations of the impact a person's actions have on the humanity of the parties involved is relegated to a lower priority. This raises, again, the ethics of surrogacy. Ethical questions gets lost if a person loses the capacity to distinguish between the map he is using and the territory he is exploring. This is surprisingly easy to do. Not falling prey to this confusion requires consciously exploring the fact that a substitution is in play, and that pursuing that substitution is a response to a strong interior desire. What is that desire? Is surrogacy the best way to fulfill it? Will fulfilling it lead to greater self-knowledge and the ability to function with more awareness in the world? How does it impact the surrounding community? If these and similar questions can be addressed honestly, then any shift in values necessary can be done, or not done, consciously. Surrogacy needn't be an obstacle to genuine connection. The important thing to remember, however, is that the challenge of bringing this off in an era where identity is mostly adopted and economics shape the dominant societal narratives is incredibly easy to overlook.

Ideological organizations ignore these kinds of questions because they are singular in their intent: to impose their perspective on the surrounding world. Questions about preying on a person's desire for belonging, about discriminating against people outside their group, or about wrestling sovereignty from an individual and substituting an adopted identity are not central concerns because they deviate focus from the task of conversion. When questions of conscience can be overridden in this way, the task of confusing something real with its representation has room to play itself out.

That means that the line between recognizing and accepting something that looks like belonging, but is a substitute for those qualities, can be crossed at any time. When people – even complete strangers a person has known less than a week – are generating good will, listening attentively, engaged in activities that look as though they will benefit others in the community, and conducting uplifting rituals that strengthen everyone's sense of belonging, the external standards of love and security most people associate with belonging will appear to have been met. Determining the authenticity of such actions requires something else: a functioning inner compass integrated with a solid sense of self. My lack of both at the beginning stages of my experience with Ananda Marga meant the appearance of such things – combined, confusingly, with a certain amount of real friendship from some in the organization – was enough to convince me that embracing the organization's surrogate family was the right step.

Surrogate families in contemporary society have ample opportunity to flourish for another reason alluded to earlier: the exceptionally difficult job confronting any family to raise its offspring well when the dominant values promoted by the larger society – individualism, competitive self-interest, economic rationalism, consumption as a way of life – work against that goal. The success of surrogacy in all its forms is linked to narratives promoting these values. Once the buzz of success those narratives promote loses its luster, the lack of substance they carry underneath their tag lines contributes to a profound level of unhappiness many people hoping for more experience. Unhappiness prompts a person to look for answers, usually outside himself, which in turn causes him to respond to anything approximating a healthy family. Family is, after all, the first environment in which he got answers to his questions. Religious organizations have known for centuries that conversion technologies are best implemented from inside something that looks like a family because it is there that psychological identity is formed, solidified, and healed when broken. It is there a person looks for security and love.

Despite the power of the surrogate family structure, it is critically important to recognize the problem doesn't lie with that structure itself. Surrogacy efforts that don't result in full-blown simulations of family structures can be just as effective as ones that do. Nor does the problem lie with the acts of inclusion, outreach, and contact surrogate families deploy to bring people into the fold. The problem lies with the fact that behind the actions of any surrogacy effort is the intentions of those who are providing it in the first place. When those intentions are to convert someone through emotional manipulation to adopt yet another false identity; when their success depends on the target not having a solid enough identity to perceive what's going on, surrogate families cross the line into unethical behavior.

Despite how effective surrogacy can be, the fact remains that every person is a multistoried individual, capable of stepping outside of environments steering him in one direction and into a completely different situation. This capacity, ironically, is what allows a person to both escape conversion and succumb to it. The important difference characterizing the former is that when a person moves in a direction more consistent with the readings he's getting from his inner compass, he moves in concert with something deeper than ideology.

The obstacles identified in these last two chapters – the normalization of narcissism and the predatory use of surrogacy – make this task challenging. Unfortunately, that challenge is compounded by another factor operating invisibly in the society: the background meta-narratives from which ideologies spring.

---

6   Huxley, p. 257

7   Banyard / Andrew Grayson, pp. 17-23

8   Ibid., p. 22. Hofling, et. al., (1966) did an experiment where nurses were asked to give potentially lethal injections to patients, and 21 of 22 were prepared to do so. Sheridan and King (1972) devised an experiment in which subjects were asked to shock a puppy and all of them did so, despite the obvious distress of the puppy.

9   Sandel, Michael, June 16 2009 Reith lecture, Oxford, U.K.

Chapter 4

Once Upon a Time

How do we determine the analogies that we embrace? Our preferences for some analogies over others are multi-determined, including by ideological factors and by prevailing cultural practices. In privileging one analogy over another, we cannot resort to criteria such as correctness or accuracy, since such attributes cannot be established for any analogy. However, we can, at least to an extent, investigate the analogies through which we live by situating our own practices within the history of social thought and by examining and critiquing the effects of these practices.

- Michael White

"The objection to Puritans is not that they try to make us think as they do, but that they try to make us do as they think."

- H.L. Mencken

My retrospective investigation of the intersection between personal psychology and spiritual aspiration had exposed two potent forces affecting them both. Narcissism and the desire for a healthy family had derailed my pursuit of self-knowledge by overriding my direct perception with the urgency of personal need.

As important as both these factors were, there was another piece of the puzzle that took me some time to recognize. Something bigger that had shaped me in ways I didn't understand. Discovering what this was became possible when I turned my attention to the cultural dimension of identity. Narcissism and family were certainly a big part of what shaped identity formation, but what about influences wider than this? What about the history and culture of the society I lived in?

Societal narratives are the most external and abstract element shaping a person's identity. External because they are created by people who exist outside a person's immediate influence, and abstract because the ideas they articulate are hypotheses based on observations over time which can neither be scientifically proven nor universally repudiated. Many voices, past and present, contribute to each such narrative. My efforts to understand the primary narratives in American society began in confusion, because there appeared to be so many of them being fought over. Events associated with each of these narratives were wrapped in story lines rife with values conflicts, violence, inspiration, heroic actions, and more: all reflective of a struggle the U.S. itself was having in aligning its identity with the narratives that best reflected its intentions. I knew that all these stories were embedded in historical perspectives, shaped by key moments and figures that ranged back to the founding of the nation and before, and to ideas exercising influence during those times. How were the seeds sown then affecting the street dramas being played out now? How did all of this shape not only how I viewed the world but how I saw myself? Had these narratives influenced my decision to be involved with Ananda Marga? To understand these questions better, I turned my focus to an intense period near the end of my time with the organization.

It was a time when I had been called to a meeting in Los Altos Hills, California. The house where the meeting was to take place, formerly owned by folksinger Joan Baez, was the regional headquarters for Ananda Marga's northern California branch. This meeting was to review the progress the state's chapters were making in their social service projects. It was also a mini-retreat: a rare opportunity to meditate and network with members of the organization outside one's local chapter.

The projects meeting involved about 12 people from different areas of the state. Each gave a brief summary of what his chapter was doing, its intentions for the future, and the problems it faced. During all of this, an Ananda Marga monk none of us knew, from Australia, sat silently in the corner observing our discussions. After a while, he was invited to speak. When he began doing so, everyone eagerly turned his attention to him, because we all knew he'd recently been to India to see Ananda Marga's imprisoned guru. The quietly spoken manner in which he began his description of this event belied something underneath the surface: a sense of seething passion mixed with bedrock certainty. It was affecting me in a strange way. On the one hand, it was appealing to a sense of a grand, uplifting vision that went beyond my or anyone else's personal circumstances. It was a reminder that Ananda Marga was an international organization, that its philosophy was being applied in many different cultures, and that its intentions to bring about world harmony were both noble and ambitious. The majority of what we'd been hearing the last several days had focused on rousing appeals to do something heroic about the awful circumstances affecting so many people. All of that was intended to be inspirational and it was, in a certain way. Attached to that inspiration, however, was something else: a feeling that all of us in the room were in a separate category from those being talked about: we were the keepers of a vision, with a responsibility to offer not just support but guidance to any person willing to receive it from us. My uneasiness was with what these words seemed to require of me: embracing an attractive but inflated fantasy, blown up by a discernible self-righteous quality intended for those of us in the room, but not for anyone outside of it. A fantasy whose fulfillment required continuing to operate from inside the Ananda Marga bubble, and to steer one's natural altruistic instincts into a larger, utopian vision the organization had. That vision included not just helping others, it meant persuading them as well. I knew that this vision was based on the notion of a world that was ultimately conflict-free and spiritually oriented. I and others in the room had already spent plenty of our time persuading others to embrace these ideas, so what was making me uneasy? I couldn't work it out at the time. I didn't have time to anyway, because the direction of the monk's talk in front of me abruptly changed.

Out of nowhere, this until-now soft-spoken acharya changed his tack. His words suddenly turned to fire. He amplified both his tone and volume, and began a concerted attack: on all of *us* sitting before him; on the information we had been conveying earlier.

We were stunned. We had anticipated our reports would meet with encouragement and, at least in some instances, praise. In my chapter, for instance, we had just organized an event in Santa Barbara that had raised nearly $1500 in a single day for Ananda Marga children's homes in India – not a bad sum in 1974. Our scheme had combined persuading university officials to allow students to fast for one lunch meal, in exchange for donating the money already paid by them through their dorm contracts for that meal – $1 per person – to our efforts. It was easy, painless, and had served as a platform for us to organize teach-ins on world hunger, nutrition, vegetarianism, and the ethical shortfalls of multinational agribusiness. Our results had been achieved in a short time frame, through hard working volunteerism, and in a way that provided considerable satisfaction to all who had participated.

None of that mattered to the monk now ranting in front of me. He had shifted from his spiritually uplifting tone to one of full-blown rage. He mocked the "smallness" of our efforts, his frustration building with every sentence. Something had triggered him to become wildly inflamed about our imprisoned guru, to chastise everyone in the room for not doing enough about it, and to bellow his discontent in no uncertain terms at our apparent unwillingness to do more.

My shock shifted to anger. How could he ignore the good news we were reporting? I wanted to tell him to shut up and pay attention to the work that had been done, to acknowledge the progress represented not just by our report but by others he had so quickly and rudely dismissed. I wanted him to respect the efforts people were making, instead of mocking them as insignificant.

Then something interesting happened. I quickly pushed my anger back into its box, only a second or two after it had surfaced. I met the rise in intensity I felt with an act of will but also an act of self-judgment. My will blocked my response, my self-judgment steered it behind an inner curtain of shame and guilt. How could I consider criticizing this man? Wasn't he a designated teacher, chosen by my guru, appointed by him to this position of authority? I noticed another thought jumping into my awareness: a rising sense of guilt about not doing enough to address the wider social concerns Ananda Marga was clearly trying to solve. In other words, I was replaying the exact content of the archarya's message five minutes ago in my inner dialogue. Then one final mental shift: surely the sincerity of this man's desire to change the ways of the world must in some way be responsible for this tirade? My job as a disciple of the same guru was to understand how. My job was to be as committed as he was to what Ananda Marga wanted to accomplish in the world. I finished swallowing my anger and retreated into ashamed condemnation of myself for even considering talking back to him – not unlike what everyone else in the room seemed to be doing. I left the room confused and self-critical.

No one in the tender beginning stages of being converted would have been allowed to attend the level of meeting where I experienced this monk's tirade. To do so would chase most potential converts quickly out the door. The shift in focus, the intensity of emotion, would overpower any sense of curiosity, not to mention the vulnerability associated with the need for belonging running quietly underneath the surface in a person seeking out such a group.

Once a person crosses a certain line of ideological commitment, however – defined by both time and the actions that person has taken on behalf of the organization – this all changes. Then, loyalty and obedience are expected, even when the organization's authorities act badly. Then, a person is expected to override any reservations he has with ideological forcefulness: exactly as I had just done.

Along with everyone else at this meeting, I had demonstrated the extra measure of commitment Ananda Marga authorities were looking for when they considered giving someone more responsibility. As a result, I had moved closer to the inner workings of the organization. Now its attitude towards me and others it considered solid was on a different footing. The loving "new testament" style strategies employed to draw myself and others closer during the early stages of engagement – the seemingly unconditional love, the security promised by being a part of the organizational family, the certainty offered by airtight ideologies – was giving way to an ugly underbelly. A cold determination that focused only on one thing: pushing the ideology out as far as it could go.

This change meant the deployment by the organization of a different strategic approach towards more established members, one with a much more "old testament" flavor. An approach relying on guilt, shame and fear to keep everyone submissive. This change signaled the organization's belief that its ideological tenets, and its personal authority, were now so firmly established they could withstand any doubts or uncertainties individual members might have. The confidence the organization had about this was based, knowingly or otherwise, on the belief that the individual courage necessary to stand up to something objectionable would now be superseded by the desire of each of its members to reach the end goals promised by the ideology. In other words, most of the techniques of exercising control over disciples at this stage relied on the assumption that organizational identity had been adopted to a point of no return. The raging Australian monk who had sent us all scurrying shamefully to the sidelines had tested this. He had relied on our decision to meld our individual sense of identity with that of the organization and to conflate our notion of spiritual advancement with obedience to organizational authority.

Accomplishing this mostly depended on the factors outlined in the previous two chapters: the extent of narcissistic injury affecting individuals in the organization, and the sense of belonging a person had gained from embracing Ananda Marga's surrogate family. Both these factors pointed a person towards adopting an Ananda Marga identity. Now, however, a third identity construct was entering the picture: an expectation that members take on the social and political mission of the organization as their own. This meant fully embracing the narrative that Ananda Marga's ideology was good for the world outside the organization, not just for those inside it. Once a person inside the organization adds this more expansive story line to his identity, it throws an additional layer of doubt, and guilt, over the top of any decision he might make to stand up to organizational authority.

All aspects of identity formation, including embracing the ideology's broader social narrative, work to create a level of obedience that has led a number of people to employ the term "brainwashing" to describe the surrendering of individual will a person engages in whenever he frames his life through an ideology. As the term itself implies, the efforts to remake a convert in the organizations' image, to wash his brain clear of old ideas, and to infuse his heart and soul with organizational ideology are expected to make his crossover permanent.

The term brainwashing, however, oversimplifies what occurs at this stage in the conversion process. It assumes a total incapacity of the convert to do anything about his situation, an assumption based on the belief that individual will has indeed been extinguished. It hasn't been.

The strategies of persuasion used by converting organizations are unquestionably very powerful. Applied forcefully, they're successful more often than not in their attempts to move people to adopt a particular point of view. In their harshest versions, they involve disorienting procedures such as sleep deprivation, sensory overload, isolation, physical punishment or torture. These things all occurred in North Korean POW camps during the Korean War, a time that led to the term brainwashing becoming part of contemporary lexicon, at least in American society.

What's difficult to recognize, then and now, is that this term could also have been applied to the persuasion methods used by authorities in the U.S. armed forces with its troops during this time. U.S. military authorities were equally intent on influencing their recruits to adopt their ideology, and to do so to a point of unquestioning obedience. They, too, wanted their soldiers to be compliant and unquestioning – to have an unthinking commitment to the ideology of nationhood. The U.S. government was no less reluctant than the North Korean government to activate vulnerable psychological states in people, control the surrounding environment, and lead soldiers to adopt a manufactured identity: one which embraced wholeheartedly a nationalist ideology and all the political goals that went with it.

Success in so-called brainwashing endeavors is only possible, however, at moments when a person voluntarily relinquishes his will to resist. The absolute contextual control administered by North Korean communists over American prisoners was, in the short term, extremely effective;[10] a captured prisoner frequently surrenders his will to any ideology being foisted upon him if doing so reduces pain and makes excruciating circumstances more bearable. It is too difficult for most people to do otherwise, given the constant hammering away at any resistance he might put forward. The world, in the process, may even begin to look the way it is described by his captors: but only when the new context he is in is being thoroughly controlled.

In the U.S. boot camps of the Korean War era the task of converting its own troops was much easier than the one facing North Korean authorities seeking to indoctrinate their U.S. prisoners. The methods of persuasion could be far less extreme. Why? Because the influence being peddled in U.S. boot camps already coincided with the belief system the recruits had assimilated as a result of growing up in U.S. society. It matched the exposure they had had to the ideology of nationalism on a daily basis. In other words, unlike the situation in North Korean prisons, the primary context influencing soldiers in U.S. boot camps during the Korean War had been doing so since

129

the day they were born. The exercise of persuasion was more an extension of a familiar set of assumptions about how things work than a dramatic change in a different direction. Exerting influence would have occurred in much the same manner as it did in the Milgram experiment discussed in the previous chapter. Persuasion is easier to wield when the surrounding context is already considered credible. Universities, politicians, businessmen and women, military authorities, and religious leaders within a particular society have a head start if members of that society see those institutions as legitimate. The act of persuading citizens is one perpetrated on a daily basis towards all that society's members.

What confers legitimacy on a society's institutions? What allows people to continue to trust those institutions even when they fail? Considering questions such as these led me, unexpectedly, to getting a better handle on the identity piece I had stumbled upon when witnessing the narcissistic tantrum thrown by the Ananda Marga acharya in Palo Alto. It took me to the idea of *meta-narratives*.

What are meta-narratives? They are grand, persuasive story lines embedded in a society's self-identity. Story lines which underpin that identity, which are heard day-in and day-out, directly and indirectly. Story lines that convey foundational assumptions a society cherishes and holds sacred. Meta-narratives are the mechanism a society, or organization, uses to confer legitimacy on what it does.

The challenge facing meta-narratives in conveying those ideas is a challenge of access. Big ideas are often too abstract to be readily accessible to everyone. For a meta-narrative to wield influence effectively, it needs to seat itself inside of smaller, more personal stories. Any form of influence increases in power the more personal it becomes. Meta-narratives, therefore, attach their ideas to the surrounding culture through their alignment with myths, legends, and heroes exemplifying what they are proclaiming. They need to embed their ideas inside the lives of well-known figures, historical events, popular texts and any experts they can find to add heft to their campaign to be considered the dominant perspective in a society. This all takes time, and effort. Meta-narratives don't just appear over night. They end up wielding influence primarily through repetition, over time, of their central ideas. Ideas that are then pounded into society through every communication channel imaginable. This repetition ultimately leads to unconscious acceptance of the meta-narrative's ideas.

When a meta-narrative is attempting to establish itself, the most important factor determining whether it will be successful in doing so is whether the events of the day work to confirm its logic. It's well known, for example, that the idea of Aryan Supremacy was a meta-narrative favored by Hitler to justify the actions of Nazi Germany. Making the case for this meta-narrative required, in part, a massive propaganda effort over time. That effort was certainly made by Hitler's propaganda team, but on its own, this was insufficient. The main reason the Aryan supremacy meta-narrative fell over was simple: Germany lost the war. No amount of propaganda could change that fact. If Hitler had kept winning battles and eventually the war, the idea of Aryan supremacy would have gained currency in the minds of those he ruled. It would have been used even more widely than it was during Hitler's ascension, as a means of rationalizing his government's policies and actions. It would have ended up inside of all the institutions of the society in some form or another.

The embrace by a society of any meta-narrative is also made difficult by the fact that events on the ground can obviously be explained in any number of ways. Whose ideas resonate the most deeply? Which abstract explanation for why things are happening the way they are seems to be "most" true? These questions are why organizations invest enormous time and resource into propaganda that builds momentum for their preferred interpretation of events. That propaganda operates before the meta-narrative gains dominance, and well after it is established. In the latter instance, its reach is at its apogee: people in government, private industry, religion, education and elsewhere devote considerable time and resources to continually irrigate the society with the central ideas of preferred meta-narratives. They do this via a daily drip-feeding process expressed through all their institutions. Successful meta-narratives end up being considered the bricks and the mortar of that society's context; the expressions of what that society values and believes in without even thinking about it. In a very central way, they define the society, providing an umbrella under which the individual narratives of all its members exist.

Once meta-narratives establish themselves at that level, their pervasiveness makes them invisible unless they are consciously pointed out. They assume a taken-for-granted quality that allows them, ironically, to be both everywhere and in the background at the same time. Their ideas appear in every corner of society imaginable: history books, television dramas, talk shows, internet web sites, religious parables, mainstream advertising, mainstream marketing, corporate success stories, etc. Their message moves to the level of "assumed truth" in people's brains, its main growth edge being young people finding their stride in the society or others new to the society seeking to claim their place.

The cohesion meta-narratives provide to a society motivates people to do difficult things. A person is much more likely to go into battle, pay his taxes, and obey the laws of the land if he feels doing so upholds national values he agrees with, regardless of whether those values reflect meta-narratives about democracy, communism, divine rule, or something else. The principle ideas embedded in any meta-narrative offer this cohesion by inviting every person in the society into something bigger than himself. Those ideas, over time, become something familiar he can count on. They assist him in determining why he is here, what his role should be, and what direction he needs to take: in short, they get incorporated into his identity.

When I initially considered the idea of meta-narratives, I conflated them with ideology itself. I later realized that despite their considerable overlap, this was a mistake. Meta-narratives are the larger ground out of which ideologies grow. They contain the big ideas running beneath the surface, the inspiring but still loosely knit together rationale which springs from key thinkers explaining events in ways that makes sense to society. They are broad and analogous, often selectively referencing stories and texts that depict individuals applying the principal values of the meta-narrative in some way that leads to a successful outcome. This invites the listener to do the same: to link his personal circumstances to the meta-narrative's broader story line. The more a person seats portions of his identity into the scenarios he hears about, the more he absorbs the broader themes of the meta-narrative.

Meta-narratives are thus the starting point for ideologies to take root in a person's mind. The invocation of uplifting metaphors and analogies greatly accelerates ideological acceptance, even though the meta-narratives themselves remain at the level of ideas, avoiding the operational focus characterizing ideologies. Because they leave this space, meta-narratives give ideologies the opportunity to rush in and interpret their central ideas in very specific ways.

Ideologies do this by adding a laser-like focus to a meta-narrative. They recognize the power of meta-narratives to inspire, and seek ways to ride on the back of that inspiration. They do whatever they can to build a particular interpretation of a meta-narrative. Because ideologies are interested in winning as many possible hearts and minds as they can, they seek to leave nothing to chance. They whittle down the grand ideas of a meta-narrative, interpret them through a keyhole and then set about the task of telling people how they are meant to perceive things and how they are meant to behave. Religious ideologies will use books that have been elevated to stratospheric heights – the Bible, the Koran – to validate their claims, conveniently ignoring the fact that such texts were well regarded in eras predating the existence of the current meta-narrative. Meta-narratives utilizing sacred texts in this way also ignore the fact that the trustworthiness of these books stems largely from their ability to convey the unfathomable, mysterious nature of the divine: not through prescribing how a person should act in every possible circumstance. The appeal of sacred books over the centuries owes a considerable debt to its poetic dimension; to the fact that its content can be discussed with other people, openly, rather than squeezed into the narrow confines of what one person believes and another one doesn't.

Ideologies find ways to redirect the imagination required to view sacred texts poetically into narrow, "correct" interpretations of those texts. One way they do this is by raising the noise around people through pounding, repetitive articulations of the ideology's internal logic. Another is by producing an endless string of rituals that emotionally excite a person but sabotage reflective capacity. Quietness and reflective capacity have the potential to provide impetus to a broader imagination; to lead a person to ethical questions; and to trigger consideration of a variety of alternatives to the interpretations of the meta-narratives offered by a particular ideology's authorities. This sort of bigness is a threat to the control ideologies wish to exert over their followers and, as a result, ideologies will do whatever they can to narrow the immensity of concepts conveyed by sacred texts into something they can control.

Understanding this opened daylight for me between the meta-narratives and the ideologies that spring from them. At the same time, it made the link between them much clearer. Ideologies were like the tip of a pyramid funneling ideas from its base in a very specific way, even when those ideas in their original form could be interpreted from all different sides of that pyramid. Leaving space for a variety of interpretations is essential if life's mysteries are to avoid being oversimplified. If a person can allow for such space, he is better equipped to resist the temptation to reduce the sense of awe evoked by the unfathomable mysteries of life to the sense of excited certainty ideologies wish to substitute for this.

Ideologies close any space that allows for a multiplicity of interpretation. They do this because of their fear of the bigness generated by the meta-narratives, and to take advantage of the opportunity the inspiration of a meta-narrative provides for setting in motion a narrower way of viewing the world. What makes the relationship between ideologies and meta-narratives difficult is determining when and where the threshold has been crossed from the latter to the former. Looking a bit more closely at the two primary meta-narratives underpinning various ideologies currently operating in the U.S. helped me to understand this better.

The starting point for this was recognizing that my conversion to Ananda Marga had been possible largely because its ideology is built on ideas compatible with those two primary meta-narratives. Both of them had been central to shaping my identity over the years. Both remained influential behind the scenes during my Ananda Marga years, in spite of the organization's Indian cultural roots. Both are embedded with strong and clearly articulated values, and reference to these values is indirectly or directly made every day by American politicians, members of the media, educators, religious authorities, and corporate spokespeople. Both meta-narratives have European origins, but assumed a uniquely American character with the settlement of the U.S.

The first is the Protestant Reformation meta-narrative. This narrative emerged in sixteenth century Europe during the Reformation, highlighted by the actions and articulations of Europeans such as Martin Luther, John Calvin, and Ulrich Zwingli. By the time of American settlement, the Protestant Reformation had already combined key elements of this meta-narrative with ideas from previous eras to put forward an ideology shaping much of early American experience: *Puritanism*. Puritanism had many different variations in American society, but all shared in common some core but narrow interpretations about how ideas seated inside the Protestant Reformation meta-narrative were meant to be lived.

The second prominent story line shaping the American experience also blossomed during the settlement period. It accelerated rapidly once the vast landscape of America stretched out in front of European immigrants to the country. Doing so pushed the ideas contained in the *Frontier meta-narrative* to the fore.

The Frontier meta-narrative, at least at the time of settlement, was not ideologically bound. It was being interpreted quite broadly, and the fact that it was did nothing to inhibit the interactions it inevitably had with the Protestant Reformation meta-narrative and the puritanism that sprang from it. Meta-narratives both compete with each other and adopt content from each other at various points in history. It's one of the ways a society attempts to get a handle on its surroundings, particularly when things are in a state of flux. Despite their moments of cooperation, meta-narratives are predominantly engaged in an ongoing tussle for dominance, particularly when ideologies spawned by a given meta-narrative seek to foist a particular interpretation of that meta-narrative onto a wider audience. The settlement era of the U.S. was a receptive period for many factors to compete for influence, often in ways that were totally unpredictable. It was a period of extraordinary upheaval for everyone in the country as attempts to establish democracy, enshrine religious freedom, seek one's fortune and, for Native Americans, make sense of the people who were settling the land – were all were playing out at once.

Because Puritanism was a well-established ideology before U.S. settlement, it had the machinery in place to influence American life immediately. Its involvement in the establishment of Harvard College, for example – where many young puritan ministers were trained – typifies the breadth of that influence. An early student brochure advised those studying at Harvard to

> "...be plainly instructed, and earnestly pressed to consider well, the maine end of his life and studies is, to know God and Jesus Christ, which is eternal life and therefore to lay Christ in the bottome, as the only foundation of all sound knowledge and learning."[11]

The puritans used their influence as widely and powerfully as they could, consistent with their utopian aspirations for altering society. Their resolute determination made them not just a religious force, but a political and social one as well. Their willingness to migrate to an unknown land reflected focus and determination. They were motivated by the desire to live in a place where they could practice their religion encumbered by any authorities other than their own. Their desire to build a "city on the hill" that would serve as a reform model adopted not just by the Church of England but by the wider American society showed tremendous ambition. All these qualities, essential to their survival in the new world, were based on ideas they considered absolute and immutable; ideas they believed to be the will of God, Biblical in origin, and essential to spiritual well-being.

When puritan ideology emerged from the meta-narrative of the Protestant Reformation, it combined key ideas from the Reformation with other, more traditional, religious precepts. Four of those ideas shaped the puritanism that established itself in the U.S.:

1) Faith, not adherence to church ritual, is what matters most for salvation.
2) Salvation is predestined.
3) A personal relationship with God is both possible and desirable.
4) Human beings are incapable of being "good." They are, by nature, sinners.

It's clear from this mix of ideas that puritan ideology had constructed a framework that could simultaneously give followers a sense of worshipping in a new way, but that their doing so would still be under the control of puritan authorities. As an example of this, during this time – and particularly relevant to the meta-narrative's emphasis on a personal relationship with God – the Bible was elevated in importance to a document anyone could turn to for guidance on how to conduct his life. Each person was to be his own priest. At the same time, it was the puritan ministry who ultimately determined what the words of the Bible meant. This duplicity walked a fine line between providing inspiration and keeping control of the congregation. The more effectively any ideology walks that line, the more successful it becomes. Extensions of puritan ideology in the form of various current day versions of Christian fundamentalism are faced with this same challenge every time they seek to broaden their influence. Their existence is but one example how, since the initial European settlement of the U.S., puritanism has exerted a lasting and penetrating influence on the way Americans worship, work, recreate, educate, administer justice, deliver health care, form community, and go to war.

One of the most enduring interpretations of the Protestant Reformation meta-narrative embraced by American puritans was the doctrine sociologist Max Weber referred to as *rational asceticism*. Rational asceticism broke with longstanding, traditional understandings of asceticism. Those understandings had emphasized keeping the temptations of the external world at bay through physical isolation, self-flagellation, fasting, spiritual study and the like. This required a monastic life, separate from worldly temptation. The radical idea of the puritans - articulated fictionally in John Bunyan's widely read book during the settlement period, *Pilgrim's Progress* (1678) - was to dismiss this approach as outdated and unnecessarily narrow. The puritan goal was much bigger: to achieve a spirituality that could operate in the middle of all the world's temptations. Spirituality not requiring isolation from society, but governed from within the person himself. Spirituality that was to be applied not just by a select group of monks but by everyone. The puritans saw only one way to do this: establish, inside each human being, an inward authority completely subservient to the will of God.

The ambition of this aspiration was breathtaking. The puritans wanted to penetrate so deeply into the psyche of every person that the dictates of their ideology would be internalized by all their followers. If ever there has been an ultimate brainwashing goal, this was it. It was at this point in its history that American engagement with absolutism first gained a foothold. It was here that the utopian notions of a perfect world were embraced not only as worthy but central to a fulfilling life. It was here that the groundwork, the experiments, and the zeal for having authority over a person through ideological means gained traction it has never relinquished.

All of this began with the puritan notion of internalized obedience to God's will. This was their central strategic objective. How did they think they could possibly achieve such total control of people? Through attacking the natural man. As historian Christopher Hill puts it:

> The preachers knew what they were doing. Their language is revealing. They were up against 'natural man'. The mode of thought and feeling and repression which they wished to impose was totally unnatural. 'Every man is by nature a rebel against heaven,' declared Richard Baxter, 'so that ordinarily to plead for a democracy is to plead that the sovereignty may be put into the hands of rebels.' Only the strongest religious convictions could steel men to face the sacrifices, the repressions, the loss involved: and it took generations for those attitudes to be internalized. 'It is the violent only that are successful,' wrote the gentle Richard Sibbes, 'they take it [salvation] by force.'[12]

This quote reveals both the aggression and totality driving puritan ideology: an attitude willing to repudiate sexual love, romantic love, the urgings of the body, spontaneity and even public displays of affection between family members. Pure spirit was the only worthy goal, achieved when a person had completely replaced his own will with that of God. The only sanctioned avenue for emotional expression was the highly charged church service, where evocative sermons aroused passion meant solely for God. The intention behind all puritan strategies of rational asceticism was to penetrate people's inner world so deeply that puritan ideology would become second nature:

> "...the great prophets of the Judeo-Christian tradition did not set out to make their favored religious ideology all-powerful and all-visible. They set out to make it like their God – all-powerful and invisible. Insofar as this ideal was ever achieved it was achieved above all in the Christian tradition – and especially in the puritan tradition[13].

It was this radical rethinking of asceticism which shaped the way puritan authorities translated their ideology into ways of exercising control over all the actions of daily living. The tone of this control was forceful, fearful, guilt-laden and occasionally violent. The general pathway was clear: subjugate impulses leading to "pleasures of the flesh" and move everyone towards a fearful worshipping of God. The enemy to be conquered was the sin present in everyone. Jonathan Edwards, the most renowned puritan minister in the early settlement era, is often credited with capturing these notions more eloquently than most on the many occasions where he preached the necessity of cultivating a fearful attitude towards sin:

> The wicked man is devoted to the commands of sin, and therefore may be said to be under slavery to it. Wicked men are very obedient servants to sin. All things in the world must give way to the commands thereof: the commands of God must not stand in competition with them, but must...be trampled upon by sin. His own interest and happiness must

also give place when sin requires it, and so devoted are wicked men to their lord and master, sin, that they will rather burn in hell forever than disobey him and rebel against him. They stand ready to be sent on any errand that sin requires them to go [on]; they wait at sin's gates, and watch at the posts of his doors, like an obedient lackey, to hear what commands he has for them to clot. Thus if sin requires them to steal, swear, defraud or commit fornication, it is done; if sin commands them to do that which tends to their own ruin and destruction, it is done; if sin commands them to run and jump into the bottomless pit, the sinner immediately obeys, and runs with all his might towards this pit of fire and brimstone. And whatever fears and dreadful apprehensions he may have on his mind, yet he is such a devoted servant to sin that it shall be performed. Thus he is entirely given up to obey this tyrant, sin.

- Jonathan Edwards
"Wicked Men's Slavery to Sin"

This quote joins numerous others uttered in puritan sermons that convey the notion of humanity as inherently sinful, at the mercy of urges that are destined to destroy him unless God himself chooses him for salvation. This became the basis for an authoritarian, power-driven subjugation of the community's behavior and mindset. The puritan belief that every person was captive to sin offered only one avenue of escape.

That avenue, of course, was to embrace wholeheartedly the guidance of puritan authorities and their ideology. The hell fire and brimstone preaching of the early puritans hit upon a simple but magical influence formula: scare people witless, then give them answers that further advance the power of puritan authorities, answers which require absolute obedience. Simple answers that divide the world into good and evil, are easy to understand, and which separate Puritanism from other influences. Far from assisting people towards any form of self-discovered mastery, the puritans were convinced people were incapable of it.

In the exercise of their authority, the puritans required none of the sophistication seen today in more media-directed means of securing obedience to an ideology. In the days of the early puritans this wasn't necessary. Members of puritan settlements were much closer to a daily fight for survival, unable for the most part to live outside the communities they forged, and not desiring to do so since they had come to the new world primarily to worship freely in the puritan way. In the face of these abundant survival challenges, the dictates of rational asceticism served puritan authorities well as a social glue to bind people to their commands. The values of Puritanism, conveyed repeatedly in terrifying sermons, could be communicated a very local, person-to-person way.

Because the level of fear community members felt ran deep, their willingness to relinquish sovereignty over their lives to religious overseers came easily. Knowing this, puritan authorities did everything possible to maintain their ironclad control over community members. Their insistence that the interpretation of the doctrine of rational asceticism should always returned to them ensured that their authority remained largely unchallenged, even when the absolute nature of that authority led to horrific abuses of power. The Salem witchcraft trials were the most infamous of these abuses. That sort of event was, thankfully, less common in American puritan society than it had been in the earlier days of European puritans, particularly when those days were being shaped by the behavioral guides of Frenchman John Calvin. Calvin had composed a manual of discipline while in Geneva - his *Institutes* - which laid out punishments for any deviation, large or small, a person might commit which was contrary to puritan ideology. During this time people were excommunicated with regularity, children were beheaded for striking their parents, torture was institutionalized and 150 people were burnt at the stake over the course of 60 years[14]. Actions such as these flow seamlessly from narrow ideological interpretations of broader meta-narratives, depending on what direction that narrowness points to and how widely its interpretations are embraced. American puritanism's commitment to rational asceticism, its belief in original sin, and its emphasis on predestination ensured that the spirit underpinning Calvin's extremism remained alive and well in the U.S.

Two remarkable aspects of this project to internalize puritan ideology stand out: its audacity, and its hypocrisy. The audacity is attributable to the utopianism at the core of puritan ideology: the firm belief in the possibility of a perfect world, where good overcomes evil once and for all. The absolutism utopian visions evoke instills people who share those beliefs with unbridled motivation – a sense of being unstoppable. Anything done in the service of an ideology's cause becomes a victory when utopian absolutism is embraced. It energizes beliefs that are extracted from a meta-narrative, cinching those beliefs more tightly, more narrowly, to the underbelly of its ideological incarnation. This intention was what lay behind the actions of Ananda Marga authorities during the meeting in Los Altos Hills, where every effort was made to persuade organizational members to embrace more deeply the organization's larger vision of a spiritual society.

The hypocrisy of the puritans was equally breathtaking. It is testimony to the blindness a person experiences when fear gains a foothold in his psyche. Plenty of examples of this hypocrisy existed in puritan days. When prominent puritan John Winthrop gave his famous "city on the hill" sermon, for example, he declared that American puritans had a covenant with God that promised them redemption in return for their faithfulness. How could such a promise be made if only God knew who would be saved and who wouldn't be? Another example is the fact that in their revolt against the authority of the Church of England, puritans went intent in setting up an even more insidious authority inside people: one that would be under their control. This hypocrisy is missed by ideologues because devotion to their cause paves the way for authoritarian obedience to leapfrog common sense, sabotaging a wider awareness that might lead to questioning the motives of those in power.

The fear puritans exercised over their congregations allowed puritan authorities to hide behind the seemingly straightforward approach of rational asceticism: the idea of redirecting one's passions towards God. This idea is, on the face of it, a logical way of focusing on the spiritual side of life. Bettering one's life, and that of the community, through focusing on spirit seems common sensical for a religious community. Most ideological tenets in religious philosophies do sound like common sense if it is assumed that 1) They will be exercised in a way that is respectful and honoring of the individuals they are there to serve, 2) They are open to discussion about how they are employed, and 3) They can be changed when direct awareness of the world indicates this would be appropriate. Implementing such safeguards would balance the pursuit of spirit with other attributes such as reason, flexibility, and ethics. This balance could then be guided by authentic, connected relationships and the capacity of a person to locate his awareness in the present so as to embrace rather than narrow his surrounding context.

All of this is ignored when ideological fervor rules the day. The safeguards just mentioned were nowhere to be found when puritan authorities deployed the principles of rational asceticism. They secured compliance from their congregations by becoming masters of a fire and brimstone theology, terrifying congregations with threats of eternal damnation and a gaping hell awaiting them if they failed to obey.

The psychological impact of such an approach is severe and destructive. Through its forcefully judgmental language, through the penalties it imposes on those who were disobedient, through its fear-based threats of eternal damnation if a person isn't obedient, the puritan doctrine of rational asceticism cultivated an attitude of deep self-loathing in members of its congregation. Self-loathing reinforced through terrifying Sunday sermons. Self-loathing reinforced through the brutality displayed by puritan authorities toward those who were disobedient in the community. Self-loathing was the fuel that enabled puritan ideology to be driven deeper and deeper into the core of each member of the puritan community. Self-loathing became, and remains, the psychological nucleus of puritanism.

The constant denigrations of members of puritan congregations, the never-absent reminder that they were sinners in the hands of an angry God, and the self-loathing that results paved the way for what ultimately emerged as the most practical dictate of rational asceticism: the Protestant work ethic. The Protestant work ethic underpins much of America's emphasis on productivity, wealth, and the drive to be endlessly active. This emphasis, according to sociologist Max Weber, was essential to the birth of another ideology in American society: capitalism. Weber saw the birth of capitalism as a direct outgrowth of the rational asceticism espoused by the puritans[15]. There was no doubting the willingness of puritans to work endlessly to establish God's kingdom in ways they believed would reform the mother church back in England and serve as a model for U.S. society as well. What passed unnoticed at the time was that submitting to the authorities driving these changes was achievable only because the puritan ambition to internalize God had resulted in people also internalizing self-loathing. The work they performed was largely motivated by the fear they had of the consequences that would arise from any disobedience they might display.

How internalized had self-loathing become for Americans, centuries after the pilgrim settlers were having it pounded into their heads on a daily basis? Was puritan ideology affecting me, and others like me, because it had so effectively become part of the way Americans view themselves? How strongly had it produced a tear in the social fabric that strengthened the hand of contemporary fundamentalist Christian ideologies, whose ideas track back to those initially put forward by the puritans?

Questions such as these expose the relationship between puritan notions of perfection and the psychological state of self-loathing. The quest for perfection takes Puritanism into utopian territory, and that is not without psychological consequence. Utopianism in any form puts something genuinely unreachable in front of a person. If a person converts to a utopian ideology, he automatically takes on that ideology's goals: including, in the case of Puritanism, those of perfection. The unattainability of perfection through a person's own efforts means the only logical conclusion he can draw about how he lives his life is that he is inadequate. When reminded of his inadequacy repeatedly, his self-regard only has one direction to travel: downward towards self-loathing. Particularly if he is subjected to sermons confirming his unworthiness, detailed laws that strictly govern behavior, and little if any reward for what he does accomplish.

Puritan authorities and contemporary Christian fundamentalists argue that the pursuit of perfection puts a premium on faith. Just because its attainment is not possible through ordinary human efforts doesn't mean it's impossible: it just means that a person has to surrender his will to God; then he can attain salvation if God decides it should be so. Faith in a higher authority defined this way is appealing because it reduces personal responsibility to one simple task: obedience to the ideology's authorities, the representatives of God's will. The current day credibility of faith scenarios stems directly from the enduring impact of puritanism in U.S. society. What isn't addressed in those scenarios is how blurred the line between faith and obedience became in the process. This is what happens when people embrace more and more extreme levels of abstraction in their pursuit of identity.

Puritan clergy who pushed efforts to internalize God recognized that doing so increased their personal authority. This happens because when a person surrenders sovereignty to any authority on an ongoing basis, the sovereignty he loses in the process – combined with the bubble he now lives in – habituates him to turn to external authority as a default response whenever his own sense of self-loathing gets the better of him. This feedback loop is closed when those authorities encourage the person to continue to seek refuge in the ideology's utopian fantasy of salvation if he wishes to secure peace of mind. By doing so, the person avoids the psychological work needed to genuinely discover his identity.

Despite the level of dysfunction this scenario represents, puritanism and its descendants have been successful in imposing their interpretation of the Protestant Reformation meta-narrative on U.S. society well enough that thousands of people over hundreds of years were, and are, capable of seriously entertaining the notion of surrendering personal sovereignty in exchange for an abstract promise of salvation. A perfect, unattainable world that depends on a definition of faith that effectively absolves a person of responsibility for his actions.

The puritans and their descendants would argue that it's human nature to aspire to perfection. This sets the stage for merging utopian notions of perfection with concepts such as original sin, in effect combining ideas of the Protestant Reformation meta-narrative in ways that leave very little room for a person to go, psychologically, other than towards a sense of self-loathing. People are then directed towards the false identity promoted by puritan ideology. Self-loathing, however, remains percolating beneath the surface of such an identity, ready to erupt into rage whenever ideological goals are thwarted by the larger society. The puritan success in persuading people to relentlessly pursue perfection as their authorities defined it has pounded the stake of self-loathing deep into the collective psyche of Americans. This sentiment is alive and well in the present day.

When I looked around and saw other cultures with different meta-narratives – cultures with stories where self-acceptance, humility and being an integral part of one's surroundings took precedence over the ideas of expunging weaknesses, striving for perfection and attempting to live in a world of pure spirit – any argument that the quest for perfection reflects human nature lost steam. Those different narratives were not, however, the stories that had shaped my identity. It was puritan ideology that had been successful enough to create a sense I and many others in U.S. society carried of never being good enough. It was that ideology that had prompted my agitated, incessant sense of striving in order to correct flaws that I knew could never, in the eyes of others, really be overcome by personal effort anyway. All the positive aspects of striving – self-development, improving one's external circumstances and the satisfaction that comes from increasing personal mastery – are distorted when funneled through the lens of puritanism. Self-development and personal mastery exist in cultures with different meta-narratives and, when pursued in a balanced fashion, can provide extraordinary fulfillment. But the puritans threw the notion of self-improvement out of balance through their emphasis on two things: 1) The pursuit of self-improvement was not to be guided by a person's own inner compass, but by puritan authorities who were disseminating the will of God, and 2) Whatever resulted from such efforts would never be good enough because only an all powerful God could determine whether a person was saved or not, regardless of that individual's efforts on earth. This steered the motivation for self-improvement directly into the territory of fear and self-loathing.

It had certainly done so for me. When I had meditated, danced kirtaan, and shared communal meals with members of Ananda Marga at the outset of my involvement with the organization, I was drawn in by the compelling components of a powerful meta-narrative that still allowed room for individual interpretation. The attraction of pursuing pure spirit, of creating a spiritual society the world could embrace, were Ananda Marga concepts completely compatible with puritanism. When I sat in a meeting and absorbed the narcissistic rage of one of its prominent teachers, that was compatible with puritanism too – it reinforced the notion that a person cannot be trusted to be good in his own life, no matter what effort he makes. When that belief is operating behind the scene, chastising people for falling short of perfection is not only acceptable but expected. It reflects the fact that the original appeal of a meta-narrative has been re-authored by organizational ideologues, which create expectations for all who have signed up to their system. The successful application of puritan ideology in small frontier communities served to provide a broader platform that eventually exercised a much wider influence as it steadily marched deeper into the American psyche.

That march did not always proceed in a positive and linear manner. The ebbs and flows in the strength of puritan ideology meant that its influence has, at times, been quieter than its authorities would like it to be. People can always break from a swoon, even one that has its origins in a primary societal meta-narrative. This was the case in 1917, when the U.S. was perceived by certain Baptist church elders as having strayed too far from the work of establishing God's kingdom. This perception generated a concerted effort to reestablish the ideology's influence. This was the primary purpose of a group of Baptist ministers who, in that year, convened to discuss their horror at the liberal direction society was headed and published a series of books known as *The Fundamentals*. This effort led to the modern day use of the word fundamentalism. These ministers were not publishing anything new, they were merely reviving the central ideas of puritan ideology, information that has been embraced and transmitted, transgenerationally, throughout the U.S. since its founding as a nation.

The history of the puritans in the U.S. raises two interesting questions relevant to conversion efforts by contemporary organizations. The first is whether the success of the puritans in gaining compliance from their congregations was due to preying on the narcissistic wounds of its congregations at the time.

The settlement era predates a more sophisticated knowledge of contemporary psychology, including the now common use of the word narcissism. That does not alter the fact, however, that narcissism has its roots in regression. Regression, a person's psychological instinct to return to earlier, childlike states of consciousness, is a strategy everyone turns to in order to cope with threat. Psychoanalyst Vamik Volkin[16], in his work on the transgenerational transmission of trauma, makes the point that regression is the response individuals in a group have when they perceive threats from outside their own community boundaries. Volkin puts it simply: groups under threat will identify more with collective identity than with individual identity if survival is at stake. In such circumstances, identity shifts from a sense of "I-ness" to a sense of "We-ness." This is true even when a person lives in an era of excessive individualism and fractured national boundaries. People need the security of the group and will turn to it under pressure even if group identification isn't particularly strong. The U.S. did this in the aftermath of 9-11.

In the early puritan era, group identification was much stronger than in contemporary times, largely because the enormous obstacles faced by the community were a daily reality. People lived in tightly woven families and communities, and were fearfully reminded of life's fragility when food was scarce, when people died from disease, or when other issues of survival had to be managed. The age of excessive individualism, and the pathological side of narcissism that accompanies it, had yet to emerge. This served as no obstacle, however, to regression to childlike states of fearful obedience in the face of the hellfire and brimstone approach of puritanism. The puritans existed well before narcissism was normalized in the U.S., but they probably functioned in a regressed state much of the time.

Furthermore, even though narcissism had yet to be normalized at this time, the self-loathing drummed into puritan congregations laid the groundwork for its growth later: when modern American society did become more highly individualized. Narcissistic behavior fluctuates between a self-inflationary false identity and the secretly held contempt a person has for his lack of a real identity. That contempt has historical roots in puritanism's emphasis on self-loathing, which takes individual psychological vulnerabilities leading to narcissistic problems into a wider social realm. In other words, as vulnerable as a person can be as a result of narcissistic injury occurring in his family upbringing, that vulnerability is exacerbated if an underlying theme of self-loathing is embedded in the culture. The puritan project to internalize obedience by encouraging – and then preying – on a sense of self-loathing in American psyches made the path to normalizing narcissism in contemporary society a much more straightforward one. It is an illustration of how the personal and cultural levels of identity intertwine with each other, for better or for worse.

The second question raised by contemporary conversion efforts concerned my attraction to Ananda Marga in the first place. Why was there such a strong attraction during the 70s, from myself and others, towards eastern spiritual groups? An attraction that continues to this day? A large part of the motivation I had for joining Ananda Marga in the first place was that everything the organization did seemed alternative to me. With the idealistic mindset of a person in his early 20s, techniques such as meditation, vegetarianism, and yoga seemed to fit well with my self-image of someone who was in rebellion against values such as self-loathing. I thought I was opposing anything to do with Puritanism. I had deceived myself into thinking I'd moved away from the predominant meta-narratives guiding society and was embracing something radically different. It wasn't until I left the organization that I realized there was more similarity between Indian guru-based culture and puritan ideology than I understood.

I became aware that Indian asceticism put forward thinking fully supportive of the doctrine of rational asceticism espoused by the puritans. Any desire of the body was to be redirected toward living a life of pure spirit, with an ultimate aim of perfection. Did this reflect common ground between underlying meta-narratives in both cultures? A religious scholar might be able to answer that question, but regardless of what that person would say, it certainly didn't take long for anyone in Ananda Marga to realize that mastering desires and emotions through either outright denial or through re-channeling them in a spiritual direction was expected. The strictness with which such asceticism is practiced increased as a person advanced up the organizational hierarchy.

For example, I was told early on by Ananda Marga acharyas that some of the dietary rules I was expected to follow, such as not eating onions or garlic, were to bring my sexual appetite under control. Yoga postures such as the *cowshead pose* were also performed to achieve this end. These bits of information were delivered a little at a time, adding to disciplines previously imposed. This denial of sensual pleasures was seen as a first step towards re-channeling energy in the direction of spirituality. Ananda Marga's approach, while different from western religions in terms of the techniques it employed, overlapped substantially with underlying puritan perspectives on passion and its relationship to spirituality. Both systems advocated an imposed battle against the desires of the body. Both systems aspired to perfection: through salvation in the puritan tradition, and through *moksha* (enlightenment) in the Hindu tradition. My familiarity with and internalization of puritan ideology made crossing the cultural bridge to this Indian view of spirituality relatively easy. Although nothing I picked up in Ananda Marga talked directly of the inherent wickedness or sinfulness of a person, it was easy to deduce that my body was considerably lower on the priority scale than the world of pure spirit when I was constantly being encouraged to override the messages it was giving me. The orange robes, the new techniques of yoga and meditation, the vegetarianism – these were all different. The underlying attitude of mastering the self through subduing it and adhering to ideological dictates was not.

The powerful impetus puritan ideology has on the way Americans go about the business of daily life is evidenced by its record of endurance over more than two centuries, and by the way its foundational ideas are largely taken for granted by U.S. citizens. American guilt based on self-loathing is on display through popular television and the wider media on a daily basis. The American desire to be a beacon to the rest of the world has leaped forward a number of times: from Winthrop's sermon, to the nineteenth century policy of manifest destiny,[17] and to more recent efforts to impose neoconservatism on the wider world. American attitudes of righteous indignation and moralizing all speak of puritanical desires for perfection, and punctuate political dialogues on drugs, contraception, capital punishment and other topics. Politicians in the U.S. are always at "war" with something, because the puritans succeeded in convincing people to be at war with themselves from the very beginning. Puritan ideology has always found a way to update itself in the midst of other influences swirling around it, and continues to play a major role in how many people in America define themselves.

The most enduring puritan legacy of all, however, is the Protestant work ethic. Hard work is held in such high regard in contemporary American society that it is never questioned. In this regard, the internalization project of the puritans has been a resounding success. Could anyone imagine, for instance, how it would feel to take an entire weekday and never actually get out of bed? To just lounge around, reading a book, perhaps watching some TV, but accomplishing nothing? Most people of working age today would be incapable of doing this without running into a wall of guilt. American society simply does not consider how the high regard for incessant activity emerged from the puritan redirection of the monastic impulse through the Protestant work ethic. Weber saw this redirection as a good thing but, in doing so, failed to see how the insidious influence of self-loathing remained at its nucleus.

> Weber's attempt to see the rise of rational asceticism as bringing with it a complete emancipation from 'otherworldliness' and 'irrational self-torture' is ultimately confounded by the negative role which the new mental discipline ascribed to reason. For the rise of monastic rationalism did not change the underlying attitude of Christians towards purity. Their spiritual journey remained as much conditioned by the doctrine of 'contemptus mundi' as it ever had been. In many respects the emergence of ascetic rationalism merely translated into mental terms – terms which were ultimately more subtle and more psychologically effective – the forms of self-contempt and self-chastisement which are found in the cruder and more primitive forms of asceticism.[18]

For all its influence, the utopian ambition of the puritans did not have the stage all to itself. That ambition had to coexist with a second, equally powerful influence, one much more secular in nature: the Frontier meta-narrative. I didn't have to look far into my Ananda Marga past to see evidence of the Frontier meta-narrative operating, and the examples I uncovered made it abundantly clear that its invisible hand had shaped my approach to life with as much forcefulness as puritan ideology had done.

The period I'm referring to was towards the end of my involvement with the organization. That was when I was asked by the political branch of Ananda Marga to participate in the upcoming *Maha* (the Sanskrit word for "great"): a training, I was told, to develop Sadvipras (spiritual warriors). The event was accompanied by great fanfare, and those selected to participate instantly felt themselves recipients of a special privilege offered selectively within the organization. I enthusiastically accepted my invitation, eager to branch out beyond my local region and make a larger impact.

The 12 Margiis who gathered in Seattle for the Maha had no idea what we would be doing. We suspected it would be intense but I, for one, didn't have any pictures in my head about what that meant. In my naiveté prior to the event, I persuaded myself that becoming a spiritual warrior had to do with increasing my discipline/effectiveness in meditation, yoga and community service projects. It never occurred to me a more literal definition of the word might be relevant.

All of us participating were briefed upon arrival. This was done by the local head of PROUT, an acronym standing for Progressive Utilization Theory, the philosophy underpinning Ananda Marga's political wing. The man doing the briefing had once been a member of the Weather Underground, the radical 60s offshoot of the Students for a Democratic Society that had its origins in anti-Vietnam war protests. Although it had been quiet for a few years, members of the Weather Underground in the past had shown themselves more than willing to resort to violence to accomplish their end of "bringing capitalism to its knees." Several of the Weather Underground had joined Ananda Marga and were making their presence felt in PROUT.

The soft, reassuring setting of meditation rooms - an environment all of us from less politicized regions of the Ananda Marga network had grown accustomed to - was nowhere to be seen at the PROUT briefing meeting. Instead we found ourselves in a small, dimly lit room enclosed by four undecorated concrete walls. It was so cramped that all of us except the speaker had to sit on the floor, our knees pressed to our chests. To track the speaker's prowling dialogue, it was necessary to hunch our necks upwards and gaze into his stern but animated face. That face and the deadly serious voice he used was as opposite to that of the meditation lecturer I had attended two years previously as anything I could have imagined. The Maha, we were told, was a deadly serious undertaking. It was training in guerilla warfare tactics.

The reason such training was needed – the reason it was essential – was because society was on the verge of collapse. Eventually, it would topple under the weight of its own greed. When that happened, there would be a need for people to step into the breach and point the way towards a more spiritual way of life. Sadvipras – individuals strong mentally, spiritually, emotionally and physically – were the people who would do this. That was what *Baba* (a term of endearment used to refer to the guru) had already written; it was what he had said. That was the path we all must walk. Because we would always be sure to walk that path spiritually, we were different from secular organizations such as the SLA (Symbionese Liberation Army, the group that had kidnapped Patricia Hearst and was demanding that profits from her father's newspaper empire be used to feed the poor.)

Leaning forward and placing his foot on the seat of the room's only chair to emphasize his point, the last thing our Weatherman-turned-Margii said to us was that pursuing spiritual life involved more than just "sitting on a pillow." We had to be able to constantly generate an opposing force; to maintain commitment in the face of omnipresent capitalist greed; to do "whatever it takes" to demonstrate to the world the importance and necessity of living spiritually.

As this passionate ideological pep talk unfolded, I once again found myself inspired. Inside, I was enthusiastically rising to meet the speaker's emotion with my own. His words, combined with the fact that I now knew I was one of the "chosen ones" selected to undergo sadvipra training, was serving its unannounced purpose of inflating my self-importance and, I discovered later, that of the other Maha participants. The grandiosity of the organization's ideology was surging out of us, riding on the wave of the speaker's iron clad charisma. "All right," he concluded, "here's what we're going to do...."

*   *   *   *

As my commitment to Ananda Marga had grown, so had my willingness to explore new horizons, and to do so with less doubt. The excitement of forging ahead into uncharted territory, and doing so without restraint, became greater than the fear of doing so. This, I later realized, was one of the defining characteristics of the Frontier meta-narrative.

The frontier meta-narrative's idea of limitless possibility has obvious connections to the physical landscape of the United States. That landscape served to advance a change that had emerged in European society when it had moved from the Middle Ages to Modernism: the idea that a person had mastery over his own fate. A growing confidence in the notion of shaping one's destiny contributed enormously to the cultural and scientific progress that occurred in Europe before people began to cross the Atlantic to settle in the New World. That progress was amplified by the opportunities triggered by the U.S. frontier: the vast, panoramic, resource rich, and seemingly infinite landscape stretching out in front of the settlers.

It was my immediate resonance with the idea of limitless possibility that had fueled my excitement when I listened to the passionate articulations of the Margii briefing us about the Maha. Why couldn't our group create a genuinely spiritual society? We were living, after all, in a country whose "can do" attitude was a defining characteristic of its history. Why couldn't inner spiritual landscapes not just be explored but mastered through enough commitment and discipline? A spiritual society and individual enlightenment were the promised land Ananda Marga used to entice its followers; it was available to anyone willing to follow its ideology. Seizing that opportunity reduced life to an exercise in will: if a person could just muster the boldness he needed, he could pull off anything.

Limitless possibility wasn't the only force affecting European settlers as they tried their hand in the new world.

Two other, related ideas characterized the Frontier meta-narrative: *individualism* and the *self-made man*. All three of these concepts were central to the theory postulated by U.S. historian Frederick Jackson Turner. His study of the U.S. settlement period led him to consider in detail how the physical frontier facing European had shaped their thinking and behavior. Turner believed that the explosive opportunities presented by the frontier evoked the meta-narrative just described. He also thought specific characteristics nested inside these broader ideas emerged during this time: vision, innovation and the willingness to take risks on the positive side of the spectrum; disdain for authority and the breakdown of community on the negative side. Through his depictions of the frontier's influence on Europeans, Turner was the first to identify that the broader idea of shaping one's destiny was already narrowing into something more specific. He was, in part, sounding a warning bell – a caution against interpreting the big ideas of a meta-narrative too narrowly. His thesis on The Frontier in American History puts it this way:

> "As has been indicated, the frontier is productive of individualism. Complex society is precipitated by the wilderness into a kind of primitive organization based on the family. The tendency is anti-social. It produces antipathy to control, and particularly to any direct control. The tax-gatherer is viewed as a representative of oppression. Prof. Osgood, in an able article, has pointed out that the frontier conditions prevalent in the colonies are important

171

factors in the explanation of the American Revolution, where individual liberty was sometimes confused with absence of all effective government. The same conditions aid in explaining the difficulty of instituting a strong government in the period of the confederacy. Frontier individualism has from the beginning promoted democracy.

But a democracy born of free land, strong in selfishness and individualism, intolerant of administrative experience and education, and pressing individual liberty beyond its proper bounds, has its dangers as well as its benefits. Individualism in America has allowed a laxity in regard to governmental affairs which has rendered possible the spoils system and all the manifest evils that follow from the lack of a highly developed civic spirit..." [19]

If Turner's thesis regarding the influence of the frontier is correct, would not the seemingly infinite landscape, so evocative of possibility for European settlers, have had a similar impact on the Native Americans already living in the country? Wouldn't they, too, have felt compelled and excited at the prospect of taming the frontier? After all, they had experienced the hardship the European settlers were facing many times over, and had already discovered ways to survive and even thrive in it.

The answer to this question illuminates how deeply seated, and how taken for granted, the influence of meta-narratives are in any society. Different Native American tribes have varying views of their relationship to the land, but within that variance there is no viewpoint that advocates the notion of conquering it. Native Americans do not view the land for the opportunities it presents; it is viewed for the sustenance it provides – physically and spiritually. The Frontier meta-narrative embedded so deeply in the identity of European settlers is simply not part of the Native American outlook on life. As obvious as this may seem, the depth of this chasm between viewpoints highlights how strongly meta-narratives influence the way cultures structure themselves, and how individuals within those cultures absorb key narrative elements into their own identity. When Native American meta-narratives place human beings as part of nature rather than as masters of it, this generates a completely different set of ideas about how a person sees himself than when a puritan tries to internalize God's authority by burning a suspected witch at the stake, or when a frontiersman clear cuts thousands of acres of forest for the railroad he wants to build. It also dramatically shapes how that person acts towards other people and towards his surroundings. Despite having knowledge of this difference for centuries, there has been an astonishing incapacity on the part of the European settlers in the U.S. and Native American tribal groups to reconcile their vastly different viewpoints in ways satisfying to both societies. This is a prominent illustration of how world views carried by meta-narratives run deeply inside an individual, and the challenge facing any person when he encounters ideas radically different from his own is immense: it's one that usually only shifts when forced to by circumstances. Those circumstances can be generated by the actions people take or by the progression of events over time. Regardless of their source, this shift needs to be powerful and sustained if it's to have any hope of replacing the dominant meta-narratives underpinning a society.

My susceptibility to the frontier-style inspirations I kept having at various junctures of my Ananda Marga experience was commonplace. The drumbeat of individual aspiration, the self-made man, and always thinking of what's possible characterizes American life; it forms a platform for much of the creativity and inventiveness produced by U.S. society. That way of viewing things didn't change just because I'd joined Ananda Marga. It didn't surprise me how entrenched my personal identity was with the Frontier meta-narrative, but the *depth* of that entrenchment took me aback. Dominant meta-narratives were clearly a huge component of individual identity. How did those threads determine what direction my pursuit of self-knowledge took? What would I have to do if I wanted to operate more independently of the influence of the Frontier meta-narrative? The link between limitless ambition and anti-community behavior characterized how countless frontier settlers had acted, and how many American investment bankers act in the present day. If I were to follow the directives about to be articulated by the PROUT spokesperson for Ananda Marga, how would I be any different to this?

As ideologies narrow the grand ideas of a meta-narrative into prescriptions for behavior, they greatly energize activity – that is their primary attraction. The primary negative consequence of that narrowing, however, is how it serves to decontextualize behavior. It does this by pushing a person in the direction of others who think as he does, whose values he shares, and who is willing to be his ally. This process is a double-edged sword. On one side is the much-needed wider support anyone wanting to effect change in the world has to have. On the other side, much closer than people suspect, is the possibility of slipping into doing so in an ideological manner without even noticing that this has happened. It takes considerable awareness to know which side of the line a person is on at any given point in time.

One way a person can tell if he's inside a bubble created by an ideology is when the only consequences he considers are ones affecting people who think as he does. It's more difficult than it sounds to think more broadly than this, because the awareness necessary to do so also requires pulling back from whatever is driving his ambitions. Another way a person can catch himself being captured by an ideology is when he starts to distort characteristics which, when the larger context is taken into account, are useful not just to him but to the larger society. Characteristics that are neutral when viewed from a larger platform, but which become distorted when they are pared down to accommodate a narrower set of ideas. Take the example of risk-taking.

When the Frontier meta-narrative gained enough traction, the primary ideological corridor it funneled itself down was free market capitalism. Free market capitalism highly values both individualism and the self-made man; it elevates entrepreneurialism to stratospheric heights. When that's the case, the risk-taking affiliated with both these characteristics is similarly elevated. Risk-taking joins the uppermost echelon of desirable cultural qualities. When risk-taking operates within the ideological bubble of free market capitalism, it does so against the backdrop of a belief that unimpeded free market capitalism produces the best possible society. Depending on how ideologically a person holding this belief acts, he can use it to justify actions that degrade the natural environment, manipulate the financial system, and unravel community safety nets. Risks taken in the service of an ideology take precedence over any consequences to people or institutions outside that ideology. Such risks refuse to acknowledge any larger sense of restraint that might protect those people or institutions. When restraint is removed, risk taking instead takes on the tone of a game. The players of such games become entranced with the game itself. When they succeed – especially if their success is big and/or comes easily – all they want to do is play some more. They become completely untethered to anyone or any institution not sharing their ideological aspirations. They just keep looking for the "action," gradually losing not only a wider perspective but the very capacity to relate in any meaningful way to people outside their game.

This type of distortion occurred with another quality highly valued by the Frontier meta-narrative: vision. Vision, as inspiring as it can be, runs amuck when it becomes decontextualized. Visions set in isolation from their surroundings have damaging, often disastrous, consequences. There are countless twentieth century examples of this, many of which are industrial revolution era projects that led to climate change consequences now demanding the world's attention. Those consequences can invariably be traced back to someone's decontextualized vision which, in all likelihood, was greeted with societal accolades when it was first articulated[20]. The difficulty required to shift gears in relation to such visions long after their downside has been identified, however, illustrates how entrenched meta-narratives are. It also illustrates why anyone seeking to point society in a different direction turns increasingly to highly emotionalized methods of persuasion to convert others to their view point: they want to shorten, as much as possible, the timeline that events supporting their perspective take to be absorbed by the wider public. Relying solely on facts to do this ceased to be enough long ago. When persuasion dominates the picture, when decontextualization is in full swing, and when surrounding events seem to confirm a narrow perspective of a particular meta-narrative, some form of ideology is either already operating or about to emerge.

Another indication that ideologies have blocked a more panoramic awareness is to notice what happens to attributes or perspectives associated with non-dominant meta-narratives. As harmful as the above examples of distorting neutral characteristics in a meta-narrative are, it's still better than ignoring a characteristic altogether. The Frontier meta-narrative emphasizes limitless possibility, individualism, and the self-made man in the starkest possible way; in doing so it pays no attention to qualities such as restraint, community, an ethical sense, or respect for nature. These are simply not a featured part of the Frontier meta-narrative, and its dominance has successfully convinced people who wish to continue functioning in mainstream society to look the other way regarding these qualities.

This happens even when people think they are operating outside of the dominant meta-narrative. As noted earlier, the rational asceticism of the puritans fit comfortably with Ananda Marga's methods for channeling desire towards an ultimate spiritual goal, something I failed to recognize immediately. I had a similar blind spot regarding Ananda Marga's shared common ground with the Frontier meta-narrative. One example of this could be seen in the organization's system of spiritual lessons. These were provided by acharyas as a means of hastening progress towards the end goal of enlightenment. Each lesson incorporated new skills: initiation and first lesson worked with mantras, second lesson with devotion, third lesson with the different powers of different chakras, fourth lesson with pranayama, and so on up the ladder. This progression put an emphasis on individual initiative no less intense than the inducements made to business people to climb the corporate ladders of their organizations. Every Margii in every chapter knew exactly how far his colleagues had gotten in the "quest" for enlightenment. Had I been expecting an organization free of competition when I joined up? Yes. Once I found out otherwise, however, I trained for the spiritual gold medal as hard as anyone. Chogyam Trungpa Rinpoche warned of this problem in his illuminating 1973 text *Cutting Through Spiritual Materialism*. That warning temporarily caused sheepishness in spiritual circles, but it wasn't enough to prevent most people from curtailing their competitive behaviors for long. Doing so is a hard task, made harder when there is insufficient recognition of how deeply embedded the ethos of the Frontier meta-narrative is.

Exploring how to prevent the distortion of ideas originating in a meta-narrative requires three things: 1) resisting the urge to narrow that meta-narrative down; 2) making its core concepts more visible; and 3) avoiding the perils of decontextualization by bringing ideas in supposedly "oppositional" meta-narratives more to the foreground. All struck me as useful in understanding better how surrounding culture contributes to individual identity.

This is not an easy task, especially at the level of the wider society. Consider, for example, the challenges presented by doing so in relation to a few recent events. How easy would it have been in the U.S. to have a discussion about the definitions and merits of patriotism at the height of the Abu Gharib prison scandal in the U.S.? Or the challenge facing the country in trying to discuss the dangers presented by climate change before *An Inconvenient Truth* was shown in movie theaters? Or the challenge facing any group wishing to discuss the proper relationship human beings need to have with market forces before the 2007 recession began? There were people who did each of these things, but their voices only received attention at the fringes of the society. All of these topics quickly became accessible when events moved them into territory where the certainty about a particular way of viewing each of them was shaken. Events, more so than any other force, are the most powerful factor capable of shifting a meta-narrative from its state of dominance. As events illuminate more clearly the difficulties society's dominant meta-narratives are facing, efforts to oppose them, create new ones, or explore dimensions of others that have been ignored increasingly become part of the landscape. This forces the key ideas of a dominant meta-narrative into the open, available for examination instead of being filed away in a category of assumed truth. When the latter is the case it allows the stage to be dominated by ideological approaches, which relegates the most important characteristic missing from the dominant meta-narratives – a discussion of ethics – to a corner of history or, even worse, to collateral damage suffered during ideological warfare.

During my Ananda Marga years I attended an event which, because of its simplicity, its straightforwardness, and the fact that it involved interacting with one of the world's best-known organizations, provides an instructive example of how seeing things ideologically not only undercuts a person's ethical sense but supports the "win at all costs" competitiveness embedded in free market capitalism. This event seems rather quaint relative to the large scale ethical violations that have been splashed across the media since the Enron scandal broke in 2001, but its transparency is helpful in understanding how cynical, and insidious, the deception employed by ideological authorities towards anyone living outside the influence of their swoon is.

I was doing work for Ananda Marga in the Bay Area in 1974, and had been invited along with several others in the organization to a "special dinner" by some people we had met during the day. They said they were very interested in meditation and spirituality, and wanted to find out more about it. As we rang the doorbell of this upscale home in San Francisco, we were greeted by three smiling young women in full-length muslin dresses warmly inviting us in and thanking us for coming. Activity was humming in all areas of the house. In the living room, for instance, a young man in a wheelchair was singing *Climb Every Mountain* to inspire his audience, who enthusiastically applauded the conclusion of his song. In another room, an older man was feverishly lecturing to a group of about 20 people, alternately addressing them and then turning to earnestly point at some drawings he had made on a whiteboard.

It quickly became clear that the interest in meditation expressed by the person I had encountered during the day had been a ruse to bring us into this supercharged conversion environment. My Ananda Marga colleagues and I stayed nonetheless, curious about how another group went about its business and confident we were not about to drop our own allegiances. One of our hosts, whom we had by now realized were Moonies (members of the Unification Church headed by Sun Myung Moon), finally dropped his concern about the direction our souls was heading long enough to engage us in an interactive conversation.

That conversation turned to the subject of how difficult it was to raise money for our respective organizations. He said that they employed a very effective street fund raising strategy. It involved putting people at intersections in wheelchairs with collection cans, then stating they were collecting for a Christian charity assisting disabled people. As we talked, it became apparent that their people in wheelchairs had no disability at all. When I confronted the person telling me this with the dishonesty of his approach, he laughed.

> "Of course our volunteers are not disabled, but that doesn't matter. You must do whatever it takes to keep people away from Satan. When people give us money, they may not realize it at the time, but they taking their first steps away from the Devil. We are simply helping them come closer to God."

My conversation with the Moonies exposed a strategy that is anything but unusual. Contemporary shell games are clearly better disguised, more sophisticated, and much bigger in scale; but nothing I saw either then or now has convinced me that the puritan belief that "people must be saved from themselves" has lost any steam in the behaviors displayed by an ideological approach to life. The ethical wasteland characterizing the approach used by Moonies on the streets of San Francisco in the 70s is employed confidently and frequently in contemporary U.S. society by politicians, corporate CEOs, religious figures, media outlets, green groups, NGOs and others. The primary difference is one of sophistication of technique, not intention. If a person believes in his ideology so substantially that he willingly lies to achieve its ends, and does so without any pangs of conscience, he is functioning as an ideological automaton. He will have narrowed concepts from a larger meta-narrative into a behavioral map that restricts valid human activity to agreement with the pathways outlined by that map. He will often be driven by a sense of absolutism about his ideology, giving him a certainty in its rightness that is immovable: an unwavering faith etched in cognitive marble. Contradictory facts will have no bearing on this state of mind. This is why ideological certainty is the foundation stone of fundamentalism. It is also why absolute certainly about anything is a death knell for ethical awareness.

Public discussion that doesn't descend into ideological silos is the countervailing force to this sort of behavior. If such discussion is to gain the momentum, it needs to widen the conversation beyond the current dominance of the Frontier and Protestant Reformation meta-narratives. One critical impact having such conversations is likely to generate will be recognition of the importance of meta-narratives in the overall fabric of identity construction. The normal sequence of identity building starts with a primary relationship, moves to the family, and then moves to the wider society. If the first two steps in this sequence have not gone smoothly, the intensity a person applies to seeking it in the wider society will amplify. He will move still further outward because he's seeking the initial mirroring relationship he didn't receive initially.

The problem with this is that the farther a person moves away from himself in his search for identity, the more desperate his need becomes. The greater the level of desperation, the greater the person's susceptibility to persuasion becomes. This unduly amplifies the influence meta-narratives have on how a person views himself. When persuasion is based on ideological interpretations of dominant meta-narratives, it serves to further patch together an adopted identity forged through intense emotion. Adopted identities emphasizing that a person is not capable of ever being good, or that amplify a sense of individualism to a point where selfishness is seen as normal, lead a person away from rather than towards any inner wisdom. When an ideological, externally adopted identity is formed in this way, characteristics of the dominant meta-narratives will be overemphasized and those that shape alternative meta-narratives will fall away. This paves the way for all sorts of distortions. It might be the distortion that occurs through a utopian ideology emphasizing some sort of final solution. It might be the distortion caused by transference-counter transference reactions.

That's why ideas such as individualism, innate sinfulness, and the self-made man have to be counteracted by their opposites: an awareness of community, self-acceptance, and interconnectedness. It's why the soaring feeling that attaches itself to the sense of limitless possibility needs to ground itself in a larger context, one that incorporates awareness of the community and the environment.

All the factors shaping identity discussed so far have opposing directions they can travel: Can a person navigate through narcissistic damage to the healthy level of self-focus needed for enduring confidence? Is he willing to fight for the rigor of a genuine community rather than collapse into the arm of like-minded surrogacy environments? Can he expose himself to the inspirational dimension of a particular meta-narrative and simultaneously open himself to what its opposite number has to offer?

To walk this razor's edge requires a level of awareness and personal courage most people find extremely difficult to muster. One of the key allies enabling a person to do so is to learn to distinguish between transcendence and transformation. The next chapter explores my own efforts to do this, once again through the lens of the mistakes I made during my Ananda Marga years. Mistakes that revealed, once again, how easy it is to mistake a map for the actual territory it represents.

---

10 Frank, pps. 154-5
11 Anonymous, p. 26
12 Hill, in Webster, p.5
13 Webster, p.4
14 Webster, p.12
15 Others would argue that the primary ideas embedded in capitalism ended up being influenced as much by the Frontier meta-narrative as by Puritanism.
16 Volkin, pp. 56 - 87
17 O'Sullivan, entire
18 Webster, p. 8
19 Turner, pps 20 - 25
20 This example highlights a huge difficulty in getting a handle on context, however: climate change wasn't even on the conceptual radar when many of these projects were initiated. How can a society possibly predict all the ways its big decisions will ultimately affect people? Prophecy is not required now, however; the difficulty society faces in putting the brakes on the damage generated by its earlier visions can no long take refuge in ignorance.

Chapter 5

Transformation Not Transcendence

"There are good reasons to believe that people like Jesus and the Buddha weren't talking nonsense when they spoke about our capacity as human beings to transform our lives in rare and beautiful ways. But any genuine exploration of ethics or the contemplative life demands the same standards of reasonableness and self-criticism that animates all intellectual discourse."

- Sam Harris

All this reflection on my Ananda Marga experience was, by now, making it abundantly clear that pursuing self-knowledge had become something I had to fight for: this seemed a strange metaphor, considering the contemplative imagery normally associated with such an undertaking. When I glanced in the rear view mirror, however, I saw that this was exactly what I had been doing since my first days with the organization. The path had been rife with obstacles I couldn't have begun to imagine when I attended that first lecture on meditation. Obstacles that were psychological and sociological, related to aspiration and self-loathing, a response to the destruction of community and the desire to create it, and driven by both an impetus to heal and to have a life in which self-knowledge continued to grow. Any of these factors on its own was confronting enough, but in combination with each other the task of sorting through the ambivalence, emotional highs, personal needs, and occasional transcendent moment they generated created a labyrinth of challenges exciting, intimidating and frequently confusing.

Understanding the impact of a damaged identity, the appeal of a surrogate family, and the underpinning influence of meta-narratives had done two things: it had clarified how many factors were in play, and had highlighted how connected each of these was to each other. I had begun this exploration because of my personal susceptibility to conversion, but I now understood this susceptibility applied much more broadly than that. To everyone? Well, to everyone who accepts narcissistic behavior as normal, or who bases his relationships on networks rather than intimacy, or who unconsciously plays out principles at the core of the Frontier meta-narrative or puritanism. Susceptibility to ideological conversion seemed to increase in direct proportion to living life the way it is expected to be lived.

Dramatic conversions – the kind seen at tent revivals when people accept Jesus as their savior – are less significant, ultimately, than the step-by-step, unconscious variety that happen when the bold initiative encouraged by the Frontier meta-narrative crosses a line and becomes blind, free market ambition; or when efforts at self-improvement become obsessive and base themselves in self-loathing. Ideology has many faces. It can wind itself into a person's life in any number of ways. What is required of a person to track all these influences and find a way forward that isn't sabotaged along the way?

Sabotage always involves deception, either self-inflicted or stemming from external sources. A person thinks he's going one way and then the reality of his circumstances hit him. What he relied on before is now unreliable. When I thought about the role transcendence plays in the conversion drama, it seemed as though both these versions of sabotage had played a role. My brief immersion in the golden world as a 10 year old had been a powerful experience but I had, as a result, deceived myself into thinking that intense moments are the essence of spirituality. During my Ananda Marga years, that deception was reinforced by the steady stream of emotive rituals holding out the abstract promise of a utopian world. In both circumstances, I wrongly concluded that mystical experiences were the essence of transformation. How had transcendence gotten in the way of the transformation I sought? What role did intensity play in this process?

This question about intensity took me back to the Maha, an event custom-designed to produce that very quality. Intensity interested me because it dominates transcendent experiences. The clarity, the sense of breakthrough, and the heightened importance it brings to the table are compelling. I wanted to understand how intensity hijacks the quieter currents pointing the way to self-knowledge. How does it overpower those currents? What role does it play in pushing personal need into the foreground? How had this unfolded during the course of the Maha?

Following the briefing talk given by the PROUT organizer described in the last chapter, the 12 of us who had come to Seattle at last knew the gist of what lay ahead. The program was to start with what the organizers referred to as the *urban survival* phase. We were to be divided into pairs for this. The objectives for each pair was to

1. Survive for five days with no money in a confined eight-block area of Seattle, using only our ingenuity to find places to eat, sleep and work.
2. Think of and execute a social service project for a worthy organization of our own choosing within our designated area.

3. Find a prominent public place for putting up some *dharmic graffiti* (words of spiritual truth) and do so prior to a final day rendezvous with PROUT organizers.

4. Arrange that rendezvous on the fifth day in order to receive our instructions for the second phase of the training: the *wilderness experience*. The PROUT members we were to meet with would be "tailed" by two Margiis when they came to the rendezvous, and our final task was to lose that tail.

All four of these objectives required intensity of purpose if they were to be successfully executed. They required us to plan, think on the spot, take risks, and to be both creative and adventurous. My partner was a man who had only been in the organization a short while. This surprised and worried me: why was someone so new being thrust by the organization into an environment that was being described by its organizers as a first stage of guerilla warfare training? How would he respond to the pressure of pursuing these objectives when he had such limited experience with the organization itself?

My concerns about my partner turned out to be unwarranted. This was particularly clear on the final day of the urban phase. We'd successfully shaken the tail following our PROUT organizers to the rendezvous, and were now receiving the praise of those organizers for having been the only pairing to have done so. The four of us were sitting on the rooftop of a restaurant where we'd arranged to have our debriefing. Our rendezvous success had involved engineering a complicated sequence of corridor cat-and-mouse games inside an office building, timing our exit precisely with the arrival of a crosstown bus outside the entrance, and then separately taking one organizer each in different directions before independently reconvening at a point known in advance to both of us. When we'd finished, we'd taken the PROUT organizers up with us to this restaurant rooftop and were now detailing to them exactly how we had handled the other objectives.

Those had also proved challenging, but we'd met those challenges in ways that had filled us with excitement. We'd solved our lodging problem by staying in a fraternity house affiliated with one I had boarded in during my first year at university. We managed to feed ourselves by volunteering to work at a local food co-op and convincing the manager to provide us with food in exchange for labor. Our social service project had involved approaching a local counseling centre whose building was in dire need of a paint job and volunteering to do that for them if they provided the supplies. They were delighted with our suggestion and, as a result, we had secured all the paint we needed to do the graffiti. We had misunderstood the timetable for this last act, however, and hadn't gotten it done by the time of our successful rendezvous. Once we met our PROUT contacts, we had to call off the graffiti because two of our Maha colleagues had been caught in the act by the Seattle police, throwing too bright a spotlight on the organization.

The whole five days had been an exercise in intensity. That intensity came, in part, from acting upon mainstream society as outsiders. There was a pride, a kind of "revolutionary inflation," that was propelling us. Our lives had truly become defined by the ideological trance we were now living, and such trances thrive when they can push against bigger forces. Another factor that increased the intensity was the fact that our intentions were invisible to society. Those outside the bubble had no way of telling what we were up to; we weren't engaged in public displays, our social service projects contributed to the community in ways that met with praise not apprehension, and the self-absorbed individualism of society generally meant that as long as a person acted normally on the outside, nobody paid much attention to him beyond that. Being invisible outsiders infused our actions with power: the power of knowing we were training ourselves to undermine society and would ultimately bring forward something that, in our opinion, was revolutionary. This served to bond us together because of the risk involved, and because confronting that risk turned us more intensely towards the Ananda

Marga belief system to justify our actions. Not only was that belief system reinforced by our actions, it was intertwining itself with our sense of agency, deepening the feeling that reality existed only within the confines of Ananda Marga ideology. My Maha partner and I began to feel more righteous in our support of that ideology: inflated with a false sense of self-importance reinforced by the adrenalin surging through our nervous system as we imagined overthrowing the powers-that-be in contemporary U.S. society and replacing them with our own authority. This idea both focused our attention and deepened our commitment to each other. All these things stemmed from the intensity generated by reinforcing a mental fantasy disconnected from a wider context.

This intensity also allowed me to closely and quickly bond with someone I had just met. The level of trust my partner and I developed for each other initially stemmed from shared desperation. We had been thrown into a completely novel situation, one neither of us had ever faced before, required to accomplish our objectives without any outside resources, and to do so despite just having met each other. These demands morphed almost instantly into a reliance on the one thing common to us both: our belief in Ananda Marga's ideology. It was only later, with time to reflect, that I would appreciate how powerfully belief secures its grip on a person's psyche when it's given credit for helping a person successfully navigate through a series of intense, frightening, and exhilarating activities. One way it does this is by lowering the temperature of the activity. The heightened anxiety my partner and I experienced when we had to contemplate doing something illegal, covert, or deceptive was absolutely nerve-racking until we discovered how calming it was to base our actions on shared belief. Belief became our substitute for thinking, something both of us found much harder to do clearly in such challenging circumstances. In managing the intensity of our tasks, my partner and I turned to each other and to the ideology. Elevating the ideology's cause set the stage for the mutual reinforcement necessary for us to deal with the fear we were both facing. At the same time, it served to embed Ananda Marga's belief system further in our psyches. Instead of meeting a situation with a neutral presence of mind, our belief allowed us to meet it with a constellation of ideas backed by a surrogate community that, together, substituted for the disappearance of our non-ideological identities during this period of heightened stress. Our adopted Ananda Marga identity, on the other hand, was getting reinforced each time we acted on the organization's beliefs in the wider world. We had completely lost the capacity to recognize that our feelings of success were only possible inside the narrowness of the ideology's self-created trance. All this intense activity was setting the stage for a mindset committed to permanent opposition, martyrdom, and a decontextualized existence.

My partner and I were not thinking about any of these things as they unfolded. For us, the strength and capacity we were discovering was all consuming. It made our belief in the organization's ideology 100 times more resolute. We had exceeded what we thought we could do, were being praised for it, and were associating that success with the wider narrative put forward by Ananda Marga's ideology. Was the strength we were feeling real?

My suspicion about this new found confidence had been aroused because there was something about it that felt...askew. Strength that comes from desperation, from competitiveness, or from being adversarial struck me as being based, ultimately, on fear. Fear of being on the losing side, of not being good enough, of missing out on something essential. A fear that had substituted intensity of feeling for presence of mind.

> "There is fear. Fear is never an actuality; it is either before or after the active present. When there is fear in the active present, is it fear? It is there and there is no escape from it, no evasion possible. There, at that actual moment, there is total attention at the moment of danger, physical or psychological. Where there is complete attention there is no fear: But the actual fact of inattention breeds fear; fear arises when there is an avoidance of the fact, a flight: then the very escape itself is fear."[21]

Finding ways to escape the present moment when it is infused with intensity is commonplace for most people most of the time. What this Krsnamurti quote led me to consider was how interwoven the inattention that leads to fear is with the constant anxiety a person with an adopted identity experiences: the anxiety of seeking externally for clues about how he should behave, the desperate quest for an internal anchor that feels solid. That desperation never allows a person's attention to calmly settle in the moment. Without that settling, ideas from meta-narratives deeply embedded in a person's psyche, or the sense of belonging that comes from seeing one's self as part of a surrogate community, or the certainty provided by a pre-constructed identity can all surface and dominate awareness. Despite how alive the intensity of the Maha had made my partner and myself feel, despite the fact that we had accomplished things we hadn't expected to accomplish, the "strength" we had gained was dependent on external validation, on a belief system put forward by others, and on being against something.

This is quite different from the strength that comes from mastering a skill pursued because a person follows his own initiative, without basing that mastery on anything other than tracking and acting upon self-arising curiosity at whatever level he decides is appropriate. If a person becomes really skilled at playing an instrument, for example, and if that skill initially stems from a natural curiosity, he will be motivated in ways that generate an inner strength unattached to any ideology. It leads him to building an identity based on his own dreamings: one in which he better understands his capabilities because he has chosen the direction he wants his life to head himself. Strength gained through self-chosen mastery is the most direct pathway to self-knowledge. This sort of strength may still be employed at some later point in the service of beliefs but if its genesis is initially inside him, it will endure over time as something real the person has accomplished in the world. This realness comes not just from the effort made at mastery but from the internal decision to engage in that effort.

Direct effort stemming from a person's own inner compass gets distorted, however, when the intensity of being against something is attached to an activity. This sense of opposition throws a person back into the ideological bubble where definitions of the "enemy" are originally constructed. The result is that any mastery displayed, including new mastery, is credited to the proclaimed truthfulness of the ideology's perspective. Direct experience gets channeled through a filter of ideas about what that experience signifies.

This redirection of a person's emerging strength brought me to a crossroads in my thinking. The building of identity for its own sake was being raided. Success interpreted through ideology was being funneled in the direction of solidifying belief and giving the surrogate community sharing that belief something to cheer about. That community could then, through its celebration of such success, override – temporarily – any anxiety a person might be having from areas of his awareness not yet captured by the ideology: ethical anxiety, for instance, if the actions just completed required compromising personal values. The surrogate community makes a false promise to extinguish that anxiety through a collective support system. That support, however, is instantly withdrawn – and the terrors of the outside world again experienced – should a person decide to step outside the ideological bubble and make his own way in the world.

Does a person motivated by this level of fear end up excelling at a higher level than someone motivated only by his inner compass? In most cases, yes. Intensity of belief is not something to ever underestimate. It ramps things up to the edge of possibility and frequently takes a person over that edge into new territory. Is there a cost?

The main cost is perspective. When a society's dominant meta-narratives spawn ideologies that exalt perfection and the unlimited pursuit of individual ambition, however, perspective emerges as a laughable substitute for the heights to which individual excellence can elevate a person. This despite the temporary nature of any accomplishment, and the damage to others that often occurs when achieving those heights.

Ideologies seek to attach meaning to any positive human characteristic by using emotional moments as an adhesive to connect that characteristic to its constellation of beliefs. They seek to convince a person that the power of his actions comes not from his own mastery, his own compassion, or his own intelligence; rather, it comes from the strength of the Christian/Patriotic/Free Market mindset he has adopted. Even actions such as spontaneously helping others, offering protection to someone who is vulnerable, or working behind the scenes to quietly remove obstacles from another person's way are attributed by ideologies to themselves, to the abstractions generated by their web of ideas. Human characteristics are robbed of their universality in this way, a universality that all should be able to celebrate. Instead they are packaged through a system that claims credit for whatever success has been achieved, further contributing to the expansion of the ideology's trance. Successfully doing this is the primary means of further securing a person's commitment, and to shaping his identity to align with the ideology.

What was interesting about the Maha experience I was having, however, was that my partner and I had initially responding to things in basic, natural, unfiltered ways. Our desire to support each other, to contribute to each other's survival, and to ensure each other's well being were foremost in our minds. Such a simple, straightforward motivation is enough by itself. It doesn't require an ideological explanation, nor does it benefit from one. Yet we gave it one. We took that next step of filtering it through the Ananda Marga belief system automatically. I found this a frightening reality to face.

Undermining my self-trust to the point where it became impossible to simply have an experience without assigning attributions to it stood in stark contrast to my mystical experience at age 10. When I thought back to that, I realized I had walked away from that experience convinced that each person already knows, inside himself, what is right or true in the situations life presents to him. That knowledge is there, inside everybody. It presents itself, however, in a quiet voice – a voice extremely susceptible to being overridden by louder ones. It can be buried under an avalanche of ideological explanations from every corner of existence, all vying for influence in the decisions a person makes. Holding fast in the face of ideological influences before identity is solidly formed is a task most people find extremely difficult. The mental noise generated by all the ideas bombarding him usually wins the day.

This difficulty was reinforced by my experiences during the Maha. Intensity had worked as a bridge to carry me from direct knowing across into an arena where that knowing gets interpreted, sometimes ever so slightly, in ways that allow ideology to replace it at the head of the line. I was also seeing how it's not just ideology that moves to the front. It's the people who claim to represent that ideology. If the ideology's authorities are successful in convincing a person that his actions originate from ideas they have already systematized he begins the process, usually unconsciously, of handing over his sovereignty to them. Ideology becomes the one-step-more-distant rationale for action, an after-the-fact explanation which may appease his rational mind but which removes him from what he experiences in the world and places that action inside a belief system. During times of great intensity, when natural instincts and ideology run closely together, the two can become indistinguishable from each other. The closer together they sit, the easier it is for ideological authorities to secure compliance. The difficulty in pursuing self-knowledge is linked to these dangers: dangers that can lead anyone to sacrifice common sense, inner knowing, and sovereignty to ideological axioms. A person usually does this without even knowing he has abandoned the task of self-discovery.

In terms of living a life based on self-knowledge, this translated to me as the need to see through the intensity associated with transcendent moments. I needed to return to something more settled inside myself: trusting my awareness, my own direct perceptions, and doing what I could to remove all the ideological filters that stood between that awareness and my actions in the world. I now understood that transformation is the work of having the strength to act upon the human knowing each person already possesses. Until that strength gains enough traction to stand on its own, a person has to find ways to resist the temptation of succumbing to ideological visions of the world: especially when those visions are closely associated with intense and often uplifting moments, or with compelling meta-narratives. Transformation operates more quietly, beneath the radar of headline-grabbing miracle moments and the inflationary false identities a person attaches to such moments.

The bridge I and others had crossed from direct experience to acceptance of ideology could be crossed in a number of ways: losing one's self in narcissistic behaviors, embracing inauthentic surrogate relationships, unconsciously adopting crossover themes from a culture's meta-narratives, translating transcendent moments through a transformational lens, or any combination of these. All of these strands stand ready to be ignited by moments of intensity, frequently stage-managed by organizations for just such a purpose. That intensity increases the likelihood that a person will, in the future, come to rely on the swoons manufactured by a converting organization to reproduce transcendental highs. All these strands can and do operate at different times and in different combinations. It depends on the person, the situation, the organization, and, sometimes, the randomness of circumstances.

Intensity that hasn't been emotionally manufactured was, in my case, even more compelling. Although my mystical experience had demonstrated to me that access to self-knowledge is possible at any time, I found it next to impossible to trust this when the experience was over. My identity was not strong enough to simply take that insight on its own merits, be grateful for what had happened, and move on. I later realized in talking to others who had also unexpectedly accessed the golden world that I was far from alone in dealing skillfully with what happens after such moments.

The aftermath dangers of mystical moments are twofold. The first is that a person comes out of it with the sense of having "seen the light" and then constructs his own ideology to help others do the same. This is the case for the many people who start up an ideology. Such people are, however, just as susceptible to narcissistic capture as the converts they collect: perhaps even more so. Their wounds are just as likely to get mixed in with genuine mystical moments. Anthony Storr points this out in his book *Feet of Clay*:

> "Whether gurus have suffered from manic-depressive illness, schizophrenia, or any other form of recognizable, diagnosable mental illness is interesting but ultimately unimportant. What distinguishes gurus from more orthodox teachers is not their manic depressive mood swings, not their delusional beliefs, not their hallucinatory visions, not their mystical states of ecstasy - it is their narcissism."[22]

The narcissistic behavior of someone who becomes a charismatic minister or guru as a result of a mystical experience leads him to create a false identity based on a genuine experience. The delusion of this false identity is the belief that he has been permanently saved or enlightened, and its power is overwhelming. After all, it has infused him with a glimpse of life he knows few others have experienced. Crossing the bridge from such rarified air to an inflationary sense of self is easy if the person's identity is less than rock solid when the event happens. The power of his experience is direct, real, and brings forward a comprehension about how things work many times deeper than anything previously encountered. The problems begin when his experience ends. It's a short step to thinking he has now been permanently transformed. He has seen the light, and believes he is now permanently the light. He confuses transcendence with transformation, and this is a perfect setup for narcissistic misadventure.

It is the claim of permanent enlightenment that always exposes the narcissistic damage of its leader. What in life is permanent? How can anyone, guru or minister or anyone else, have the arrogance to claim to be "perfect," "saved," or "enlightened"? To have all the answers beyond the questioning of his fellow human beings? Yet this is what many religious and spiritual authorities from all traditions have claimed through the centuries.

To claim enlightenment or salvation to others is the most public form of narcissistic inflation possible, a precursor to the world's most dramatic and harmful shell game. It inflates the ego into a swelling bubble of delusional isolation, a bubble waiting to be popped. Invariably it is, because the identity anyone assumes in a state of narcissistic inflation is a false one. It's narcissism that was there before, and it hasn't evaporated just because a visit to the golden world has intervened.

If a person experiences an arbitrary mystical moment and is not interested in starting his own organization, as I was, he is still susceptible to a second aftermath danger. That is the danger of dropping everything else in life and doing anything he can to repeat his experience. The attraction of this is obvious when considering the qualities of a mystical experience. William James describes four such qualities:

1. *Ineffability*: The experience can't be described in words.
2. *Noetic*: Knowledge about 'how things work' comes to the person, creating a sense of profound insight.
3. *Transiency*: The experience ends, although the memory of it doesn't.
4. *Passivity*: During the experience the person feels guided by something larger than his own ego. Afterwards, he usually concludes this something is the "will of God."[23]

Others have added to this list, including a sense of *unity* with the surrounding world, and the *suspension of time* during the experience. All six of these characteristics had been part of my experience as a 10 year old. Who wouldn't be interested in reproducing an event that had these characteristics?

The unquestionable allure of such experiences doesn't address the issue of whether pursuing them is ultimately transformative. I had already learned much about how the urgency of psychological need can gum up the works, and it seemed as though there was more than just the attraction of repeating the experience in operation here. The clue I sought came through reading James and zeroing in on his fourth characteristic of the golden world: passivity. The attraction of surrendering to forces beyond the ego, being carried into something larger. Surrender, letting go of the ego, clearly required some form of passivity.

The encouragement to do this in Ananda Marga was strong. One of the rituals people in the organization learned at the stage of the second lesson given to them by their acharya was to sing a song of surrender after meditating, facing a picture of the guru on the meditation altar while doing so. At the conclusion of this song, entitled *guru puja*, the meditator was to prostrate himself face down in front of the picture. The explanation given was that the surrender was not to the personhood of the guru, but to what his perfection symbolized: cosmic union with everything, an enlightened state of being. This ritual, in other words, promised progress towards the state of consciousness already possessed by the guru if a person could successfully cultivate an attitude of surrender.

The problem with such an exercise lies in the fact that most people lack a solid, fully formed identity to surrender in the first place. Surrendering an identity that has yet to be discovered is a detour sign allowing a person to avoid the psychological work of identity formation. Guru puja and other rituals of surrender offer a "short cut," a direct line to cosmic consciousness. That's enticing to anyone who believes in the possibility of perfection. The destination it takes a person to, however, has less to do with cosmic consciousness and much more to do with a passivity that leads to compliance to an organization's authority. A person will only be able to stand up independently to such authority if he has established a solid identity.

This process became clearer to me when I came across some writings by Ken Wilber on the "pre-trans fallacy"[24].

> "In any developmental sequence, growth will proceed from pre-X to X to trans-X…Because both pre-X and trans-X are, in their own ways, non-X, they may appear similar, even identical, to the untutored eye. This is particularly the case with pre-personal and transpersonal, or pre-rational and trans-rational, or pre-egoic and trans-egoic. Once these two conceptually and developmentally distinct realms of experience are theoretically confused, one tends either to elevate pre-personal events to transpersonal status or to reduce transpersonal events to pre-personal status. This is the pre-trans fallacy…."

The pre-trans fallacy plays out in two directions. The first is that of misinterpreting transcendent or transpersonal experiences as regression. This was Freud's mistake, shared by many today, and is called PTF-1 by Wilber. Freud considered all transcendent experiences as narcissistic regression, a leap backwards to a pre-egoic security rather than forward into mystical awareness. When his colleague Romaine Rolland wrote to him to say that oceanic feelings of unity with the world were the origins of religious sentiment, Freud responded by attributing such feelings exclusively to regression to an infantile state; an adult returning to childhood so he could once again be at his mother's breast[25].

William James, however, cautioned against discounting transcendent experience in this way. He doubtless would have thought Freud was engaged in a psychological version of what he called "medical materialism":

> "Medical materialism finishes up Saint Paul by calling his vision on the road to Damascus a discharging lesion of the occipital cortex, he being an epileptic. It snuffs out St. Theresa as a hysteric, St. Francis of Assisi as an hereditary degenerate. George Fox's discontent with the shams of his age, and his pining for spiritual veracity, it treats as a symptom of a disordered colon. Carlyle's organ-tones of misery it accounts for by a gastro-duodenal catarrh."[26]

The opposite problem, the one I had fallen prey to and which converting organizations depend on, is PTF-2. This is where pre-personal experiences – experiences that occur before a person has a solid sense of ego or identity - are elevated to the status of mystical experience. It's in the opposite direction of PTF-1, but just as fallacious. I knew my transcendent experience as a 10 year old was real, but my pursuit of emotional highs that would satisfy my personal needs was misguided. It was never going to lead me to another experience with the same qualities as my initial one. What my efforts to "surrender" during Ananda Marga's emotive rituals did was encourage regression, a pre-personal state of consciousness leading to my increased susceptibility to deeper levels of ideological conversion and organizational compliance.

This led me to question all the techniques I had been learning in Ananda Marga, including meditation and yoga. They were all devoted to this notion of surrendering the ego. This was now traveling too close for comfort for me to the self-loathing of the puritans, and to the rejection of the natural self in the service of perfection. Self-loathing and rejection of the natural self both gain traction more easily when a person is regressed. How capable was I of distinguishing a PTF-2 swoon from genuine receptivity? How much of my motivation was external, how much directed by my own inner compass? Could I sustain the necessary solidity of identity to be comfortable with my own imperfections?

On the other hand, I saw the value of letting go of the ego, because of the memory I carried of the golden world. I knew there was a larger reality, a non-personal but fully alive reality. Because I hadn't done anything in particular to bring it forward, I had concluded it was available to anyone. If the impact on others having such experiences was at all similar to mine, not having a solid identity when such moments happen is a genuine obstacle to self-knowledge. Trying to drop the ego before it has had a chance to establish itself struck me as a way of avoiding the difficult work of being fully in the world, warts and all. Even if identity is ultimately illusory, isn't the fact that a person believes he has one worthy of some form of attention other than that trying to overcome its existence? What is there to fear from developing the ego – except, perhaps, that those who do so might become independent minded enough to challenge an organization's authorities? Was this the reason why there weren't many spiritual organizations placing value on identity development?

The rationale given in spiritual organizations for avoiding the work of identity development is twofold: 1) Becoming "attached" to the ego will bog down the progress of the spiritual aspirant, and 2) The ego is a restricted state of consciousness incapable of enlightenment. The first is a way of avoiding working through – rather than around – the problems that come with attachment. Attachment to the roles and functions of ego is a symptom of the desperation characterizing the identity-hopping process of narcissism; it's what happens when identity is adopted externally for the sake of others rather than discovered directly by a person. Breaking this cycle requires a person to discover who he is in the same way a child who has successfully navigated through the narcissistic phase of development does so: through experimentation done in a context where he is given honest feedback by trusted others. It is the last element of this equation that is the most crucial: we need each other if we're to discover who we are. Identity cannot simply be sidestepped by condemning attachments and trying to walk into a level of awareness free of ego altogether. Doing so reflects an avoidance of the hard work necessary for self-discovery, and the broader context required to do so.

The second rationale depends on convincing a person of an ultimate goal, a life beyond the one he is actually in. It's true that the ego is geared towards earthly realities rather than mystical ones, but that's the hand every human being is dealt. Until a person does what's necessary to build a solid sense of self, he will be susceptible to PTF-2: mistaking pre-personal states of consciousness for transpersonal ones. A strong identity provides a necessary foundation for a person to remain grounded in the aftermath of any mystical experiences he may have. Building one is less glamorous, more gradual, and more interactive than the individual pursuit of salvation or enlightenment is, but any efforts to avoid this work will ultimately dead-end his progress.

I began considering this at a time when I was increasingly operating outside of my conversion swoon. My critical thinking was reemerging through efforts to sort through all the events I had experienced, which in turn were helping me understand the state of continual cognitive dissonance I had had during all those moments in Ananda Marga when I was forcing myself to embrace the ideology. When Stanley Milgram's experimental subjects experienced cognitive dissonance as they agonized about whether to shock another person screaming in agony, the large majority of them went ahead and administered these shocks. They attributed their compliance to the directives of an outside authority. What about that minute percentage of people who didn't? I think those who were able to stop were people who had enough ego-strength, who had successfully navigated through the narcissistic phase of development, and/or whose family and community life was authentic enough (especially the ability to work through conflicts in respectful ways) that they could make a rational decision based on a critical thinking capacity. This is exactly the state of consciousness ideologues want their potential converts to avoid. It is a state of consciousness where a person exercises genuine sovereignty over his life.

One thing a person who exercises genuine sovereignty over his life is able to do is put James' notion of passivity into perspective. Should an arbitrary mystical experience takes place, the passivity James refers to above will occur in the experience itself. The person becomes a fascinated observer unintentionally, carried along by the moment, compelled to do so by the obvious operation of larger forces. Consciously letting go often isn't even part of it; the experience just overtakes his personality whether he likes it or not.

This is completely different from the pre-personal passivity employed strategically by a person who seeks a transcendent experience but is unknowingly driven by his desire for belonging and identity. This sort of passivity is identifiable by its dissociated, "yearning" quality. It's the passivity coveted by ideological authorities because they recognize it as the precursor to the compliance they seek. Learning to distinguish between passivity based on personal need and openness to experience stemming from a solid identity is only possible when such an identity already exists.

All of this was clarifying the extent of the damage that occurs when transcendence is equated with transformation. The desire for the former deflects a person away from the ongoing process necessary for the latter. Building identity involves transforming one's self repeatedly. It requires switching awareness back on whenever it's been shut off, making changes that resonate with a person's inner compass, and doing so in the context of ordinary, day-to-day living. Transcendence tricks a person with a less-than-solid identity into forgetting these simple things.

Does this mean that the emotionally intense experiences manufactured by organizations to trigger transcendence are useless and/or malevolent? No. In ethical and professional hands, the breakthroughs that can occur at such moments can be tipping points for a person that accelerate the transformative process. In the 80's, I worked in Colorado as a team building and leadership consultant. We had a name for the emotionally intense experiences we manufactured: *predictable miracles*. Our predictable miracles were rock climbing and other adventure-based activities we conducted for our community and corporate clients. While this description sounds – and is – somewhat cryptic, it is also accurate. We knew that once a group of people was on the rock face, confronting their fears, having to depend on others in combination with their own internal resources to work through those fears, a certain percentage of them would genuinely "break through" something. This happened repeatedly – a person would find his way to resources he didn't know he had, and make a number of discoveries about his life in the process.

The aftermath of such an experience is emotional, and often beyond the capacity of the person having it to skillfully contain within the boundaries of his old identity. In such a shaky state, the person needs a reliable, trustworthy support system around him that can debrief the experience and help him put it into perspective.

From an ethical standpoint it's critical that the perspective the experience is put it into is not an ideological one. Manufacturing miracles requires the greatest of care on the part of those doing the manufacturing. They need to proceed knowing that what the participant has just done may inspire him, confuse him, elevate him, regress him, or produce any number of unpredictable feelings. More often than not, the experience will have pushed the person, temporarily, into a more egoless state of consciousness. This state of consciousness is highly malleable, one where his critical faculties will not be functioning at their peak despite the influx of insight he may be having. If a person is having such an experience and his well being is not foremost in the minds of those conducting the exercise, the result can be incredibly damaging. Not only will he fail to access the deeper self-awareness required to travel further on the road of transformation, he may regress into a pool of unresolved trauma, self-loathing and various other obstacles. Despite the potential harm that can be done in such situations, the necessary caution required to facilitate a person through such an experience doesn't even occur to the majority of people inside converting organizations – secular or spiritual. As noted earlier, people interested in conversion have little or no awareness regarding the pitfalls of transference, apart from ways to take advantage of the vulnerability it exposes by enmeshing their targets more in an ideological perspective.

Prior to the Maha, when I was funneling any vaguely intense experience I had through an ideological lens, I thought doing so would take me closer to self-knowledge. The battle line in this effort, the Achilles heel I still had in terms of my conversion susceptibility, was the second aftermath danger: seeking to endlessly reproduce the high of my experience at age 10. I was looking for predictable miracles, hoping I might find them through meditation, yoga, or surrendering my ego to a picture of an Indian railway clerk I had never even met. In the process, I was avoiding the work of constructing identity through facing the challenges of daily living. I was willing to do virtually anything to repeat my experience, including tossing my hat into any cult/religion/substance that looked as though it could take me back to something that even vaguely approximated my earlier experience. If translating my experiences through an ideology increased the odds of doing so, that was fine by me.

As I worked though all of this, it raised a new question: What was I to do with the information I now had that transcendent experiences produced the vulnerability preyed upon by ideological organizations to convert people? I could not, as Freud had done, dismiss my mystical experience as merely a regressive misadventure. It had been anything but that. Pursuing a repetition of that experience, however, now seemed a fool's errand – despite the fact that mine had happened completely outside my narcissistic wounding, completely outside the meta-narratives, and completely outside any need I had for a surrogate family. All of those elements had come into play after the fact.

I knew that both predictable miracles and accidental transcendent experiences can tip a person into becoming a believer, into making what the philosopher Soren Kierkegaard first called a *leap of faith*. That seemed obvious now, and at the root of my attraction to intensity. Predictable miracles are compelling ways to get people to either stay in an organization or get them to join that organization. So are genuinely transcendent moments not under the control of anyone. Both share the fact that they are moments when the ego is broken through, insight rushes in, and the possibility of an expanded new identity emerges. Both are characterized by enormous amounts of intensity. This is not to say that if a person is levelheaded he can't use such experiences, and the inner knowing that comes with them, as an impetus to transform his daily life and relationships.

My problem during my Ananda Marga years was that I was anything but levelheaded. When I reflect back on my response to that first lecture on meditation, for instance, it wasn't difficult to pinpoint how I had overlaid my psychological needs on top of the memory of my encounter with the golden world. I ultimately saw that the characteristics of the latter – the unity with life, the knowingness, the timeless elevation of my awareness, the joy – were being *mimicked* by Ananda Marga rituals rather than actually occurring in the moment. I was identifying something by its shadow rather than by its realness.

Confusing genuinely transcendent moments with emotionally manufactured ones is a mistake made over and over again by people, and more often than not leads to that person basing his life on whatever ideology he associates with those emotions. Conversion dynamics are an interlocking process contributed to by both parties and working against genuine transformation. Transformation is an individualized matter, bound up not only with the person's spiritual impulse but also with his life history, his psychological makeup, his relationships, and the narratives of his times.

Reading James had reminded me of another key point about the transcendence/transformation labyrinth: transcendent experiences, even genuine ones, are transient. No one is permanently enlightened. Every person inevitably returns to the ego structure he had before such experiences, despite the allure of terms such as "salvation," or "moksha." Followers of gurus and fundamentalists of all varieties will argue against this, claiming their leader has done something permanent. This is nothing other than the logical conclusion of puritanism and other utopian systems: the false belief that perfection is attainable.

The consequence of understanding the falsity of the idea of permanent enlightenment reinforced the recognition that while all the various conversion factors discussed here make it difficult for a person to remain clear-headed, that difficulty is compounded when transcendent experiences are thrown into the mix. The person links those experiences to the organization via a variety of intensity pathways embedded in the techniques, rituals, and authorities in that organization. He begins to hope, and imagine, that immersion in the organization will offer him the opportunity to recreate the truest, most exhilarating moment of his life. Buying into the notion that the head of the organization has already arrived at such a destination raises that hope and generates an excitement that gives real pause to the idea of departing. Again, genuine experience gets itself mixed in with psychological need, human foibles displayed by organizational authorities are ignored or tolerated, and an effort to keep irrational hope alive is made at every turn. Sifting through all this becomes a journey through a nightmarish maze: a necessary maze, but one that dead-ends at every turn.

As I reflected upon it further, I recalled other examples of how this confusion had captured me and embedded me more deeply in the organization. One example was the ecstasy of belonging I experienced dancing kirtaan with others for hours at a time. At one Ananda Marga retreat, a 100 or so of us danced in one hour shifts for 24 straight hours, chanting the whole time. You could, however, dance longer than that if you wished. I chose to do so, for what felt like about two hours. When I checked the clock after finally stopping, however, it turned out I had danced for eight hours. This experience was both intense and intoxicating, including a feeling of wonderful connectivity with people around me at the time – much like current descriptions given by people of raves. The pleasure of it was astounding. How does such a "high" translate relationally in the long term? It translates perfectly well if both parties in the relationship continue to share an ideological bias. Not well at all, however, if one of the parties breaks away from the ideological belief system. It seemed obvious to me after my departure from Ananda Marga that beyond the transcendent buzz characterizing moments such as collective kirtaan, genuine intimacy involved the nitty gritty of working through difference, committing as long as possible to others even when you disagreed with them, generating a fearless quality that could stand up and laugh after having a false self-image knocked around, and doing what is needed to stay both open-minded and independent in the midst of emotional storms. This sort of depth never gets traction in the surrogacy environments that organizations pass off as loving because no one operates outside of the ideological overlay. If a person operates inside an ideology all the time, he is removed from the direct experience at the core of both intimacy and self-knowledge.

After the Maha's urban phase, my will began to assert itself and quietly point me in a different direction: one of my own choosing. My desire to consciously step away from my narcissistic wounding, away from the surrogate family around me, and away from the more invisible influences of the meta-narratives was reasserting itself. I still felt on shaky ground, however, as the 12 of us headed out for the wilderness phase. I found myself reviewing what I knew about Ananda Marga.

I knew that the organization had a history of confrontation with the government of India. I knew the guru was a political prisoner there, and had been for some time. I knew that several Ananda Marga monks had dramatically self-immolated to protest his imprisonment. Three so far? I couldn't remember. Perhaps my faulty memory could be attributed to the fact that this information was disturbing me at a profoundly deep level. I had filed it in my head, buried under efforts to fulfill ideological requirements but, in doing so, had staked out ground for a raging internal conflict that never abated. Years later, at this moment of reflection, the depth of this particular file drawer astounded me. Why was I continuing to push such information out of my consciousness? Would I ever act on it and challenge what was happening inside the organization?

Philip Zimbardo, whose simulated prison experiment in 1971 explored the impact of unequal power in human relationships, expanded his thinking on this issue in his later book, The *Lucifer Effect*. Zimbardo's guiding question for the book was an exploration of what prompts seemingly good people to act in evil ways. He makes the point that the line between good and evil actions is a permeable and moveable one. What affects it are 3 factors: 1) The disposition of the individual, 2) The situation he is in, and 3) The larger systemic context. While my concern here is with ideological conversion rather than the dichotomy between good and evil, I saw this framework as compatible with the ideas I had been exploring. Narcissism as a disposition prevents a person from viewing the world beyond his individual circumstances, and can easily lead to inappropriate passivity and/ or inflation. Particularly so if the situation he is in includes some degree of surrogacy, where all the social reinforcement is directed towards the common adoption of an ideology. That surrogacy can take a million different shapes: from the foxhole camaraderie of prison guards at Abu Gharib to the bonhomie of Wall Street traders. The larger meta-narratives are the powerful systemic forces invisibly influencing the way a person structures his life, frequently reinforcing ideological perspectives about how things work. The task facing anyone interested in self-knowledge is much more difficult when these factors are unconsciously embraced.

Zimbardo states that breaking out of this trance requires a person to act socio-centrically rather than egocentrically. Until a person's ego is on solid ground, however, sincerely acting in a socio-centric way is extremely difficult. For this reason, I was unable to call a halt to my involvement with Ananda Marga when I was having some of these insights at the rooftop debriefing with PROUT representatives after the urban phase of the Maha. I couldn't yet. The river of adrenalin generated by my partner's and my success was roaring through my consciousness; it took all my concentration just to stay afloat in my little raft of ego. To do otherwise would have required me to confront the organization's philosophy, leadership and purpose on the heels of the most exhilarating experience I had had in Ananda Marga so far: something I didn't feel strong enough to do, despite the emergence of these insights. My doubts about the organization had grown, but I put them to the side yet another time. My task now was to do as well as I could in the wilderness phase of the Maha.

On the ferry ride over to the Phase Two start point, a peninsula jutting out into Puget Sound, I found my reflections taking still another U-turn: one of those clever ways the mind works to sabotage a person's inner compass and discourage him from acting boldly despite sensing what is needed in a situation. This U-turn swung the pendulum to the opposite extreme. Wasn't the excitement of the Maha and being in Ananda Marga more fulfilling than anything else that had happened in my life? Why was I complaining? My meditation practice was humming along - easier and quieter than it had ever been, accessing what felt like deeper and deeper layers of consciousness. My sense of kinship with others on the program was deepening. We all seemed to be sharing a growing pride in our separation from mainstream society. Our sense of aliveness compared to the trapped and lifeless commuters we were sitting next to on this very ferry ride was a case in point. Hmmm...

When we all finally arrived at our designated gathering point, we were driven to a campground and then briefed regarding our first task on the wilderness phase. In the darkness before tomorrow's dawn, we were to illegally enter a closed area of a nearby park, which bordered a seldom-used lake. This would involve breaking off the lock on the entrance gate and, as quietly as possible, entering the area and launching six canoes we had brought with us onto the lake. We were then to paddle our canoes equidistant from each other and form a circle on the southern third of the lake. The purpose of all of this was simple: in order to have food for the next four days, it had to be air dropped by our support team back in Seattle. We were now expected to telephone them in order to arrange the exact time tomorrow morning this was to occur, as well as the coordinates for the drop. We would designate the target for the airdrop by lighting flares from our circle of canoes; the food was to be parachuted into the center of that circle.

After making the necessary phone calls to confirm all of this, we slept a restless sleep. Early the next morning we awoke and began to put everything in motion. We broke into the park, launched our canoes, positioned ourselves around the lake, and waited - shivering from both the cold and from our excitement. Within minutes the drone of a plane's engines could be heard beyond the northern ridge. We lit the flares and peered skyward at the small, twin-engine plane making its way over the horizon. Unfortunately, the Margiis on board were not particularly well practiced in the art of chucking things out airplane doors in a timely fashion. In their excitement (and probably in their fear of mistiming the drop altogether), they pushed everything out the door far too early.

Our parachuted food supplies were descending, but on the opposite side of the lake. In a matter of minutes, they would be hitting the water and slowly sinking! Like characters in the middle of a slapstick comedy, we all began paddling furiously to save our sustenance for the next four days. Our frantic efforts were successful, but we were aware that our overall skill in executing this maneuver was not about to win us rank as sadvipras.

The next few days saw us undertake some serious hiking to high mountain regions. At one point each of us was isolated inside a small, confined natural area for a 24-hour solo experience. There was nothing about this experience that a person wouldn't encounter on a well-structured Outward Bound program. Being physical challenged and hanging in there was clearly the main point. We were well and truly exhausted when, after the final hike out, we gathered round a campfire to learn how this phase would end. I'm sure I wasn't the only one hoping it would involve nothing more difficult than taking a seat in a van for long ride back to Seattle.

Far from it. We had scarcely finished our evening meal when out came the maps of Puget Sound, along with a final set of instructions. We were told that although we were exhausted from our experience in the wilderness, we should look at the previous four days as preparation. Preparation for tonight.

Our organizers pointed out that there were 30-odd miles between where we were at that moment and the public dock in the center of the Seattle waterfront business district. The time was now 7:00 p.m., and the goal was to reach that dock by 8:00 a.m. tomorrow morning. In order to do that, we'd have to set off in our canoes right now and paddle through the night: no sleeping, short rests only, all attention focused on the task of reaching our destination on time. A chilly night had been predicted by forecasters, and the currents would be against us for the duration of the journey. We would have a map and a bit of light from the moon to navigate by, and until the morning hours there was unlikely to be much traffic on the waterways.

By then, we were all too accustomed to such surprises to question them. We simply brought our canoes down to the water's edge, loaded up and headed out. The night was one of groaning fatigue mixed with moonlit beauty. We trudged, slowly, towards deeper and deeper levels of exhaustion. The chop and currents in the water made it seem at times as though we were traveling backwards. On top of this, it began to rain about four hours into our journey. Combined with the night's descending cold, this forced us ashore to find a local bar where we could warm up one of our members who seemed frighteningly close to hypothermia. Our tiredness made us all susceptible to physical collapse, but everyone was hanging in through pure determination.

As the hours passed the dawn gave way to a more fulsome morning light and we rounded our final bend. There, in the distance, was the vast and bustling Seattle harbor. Despite all the fatigue, all the pain, all the dull repetition of a night spent repeating the same motion over and over again, the sight of that skyline had an amazing impact. It filled us with a sense of exhilaration. Our tiny canoes, dwarfed by passing ferries and an outgoing Russian grain ship, inched towards the industriousness of a city just beginning to find its morning rhythms. Overhead, a police helicopter noisily passed over to determine who and what we might be, concluding, it would seem, that we were no immediate threat to the city's security.

Another hour or so after that first sighting, we arrived at the Seattle public dock. There to meet us were other members of the PROUT team, smiling and welcoming us. One of them had a newspaper with them. I glanced at it briefly and couldn't fail to notice the irony of that day's headline:

"Patricia Hearst Captured"

* * * *

It was not long after the Maha that I ended my relationship with Ananda Marga. The return to my position at world headquarters in Denver confirmed this decision, as did a

"Maha Two" experience some months later. My decision solidified as I saw more clearly that these trainings were clearly preparations for violence. This, I concluded, was too central to the fabric of Ananda Marga. It overrode all the benefits of its spiritual practices. I did not want to be associated with any organization training people in what these days would be considered terrorist methods. What had allowed me to break away from the ideology I had embraced for two+ years?

More than anything it was the memory of my experience as a 10 year old. I now recognized that the only thing more dysfunctional than my desperation to replicate that state of consciousness again was to ride on the back of an ideology in order to do so. This was the easy way out of the transformation I needed to undertake. I had to operate outside of psychological need, outside of authoritarian directives, and outside of the surrogate intimacy that evaporated when shared belief was missing. It was clearly time to leave. I walked away from Ananda Marga, without anyone stopping me.

Despite my decision, I was anything but from clear-headed about my next steps. Over the course of the last few years, I had dissociated myself from any community that was not related to Ananda Marga and was now very much on my own. I had no idea where I would live, how I would earn money, etc. The only starting point I had to reenter mainstream society was my sister, living in the aptly named Lone Tree, Iowa. When she was in the midst of divorcing her husband back in the days before I had joined Ananda Marga, I had offered her refuge living with me while I attended university in Santa Barbara. She had accepted until she got herself back on her feet, and was now only too willing to return the favor. So off to Iowa I went to live with her and her new partner.

Despite the fact that my involvement with Ananda Marga was over, I was still a creature of habit. In amongst the cornfields of Iowa, I continued to rise at 5:00 in the morning, meditate, do yoga every day, and read spiritual literature. What else was I to do? I had been living my life inside a bubble, and now that I was outside of it I was completely at a loss. I looked around for jobs, but my heart wasn't in it. Despite the hospitality offered to me by my sister and partner, Iowa was not for me. I made the decision to go back to California and remake my life in Santa Barbara. I gathered my belongings and hit the road.

When I arrived back in California I was on a shoestring budget, but was able to find a room in a house in Isla Vista, the college town next to the university, for $60 a month. For several weeks, I passed the time walking the two dogs belonging to the owner of the house, an extremely obese woman who found walking any distance beyond 100 yards difficult, and who had the odd habit of cooking French fries in the kitchen while naked. The Doberman, Beagle, and myself soon became fast friends, as the three of us wandered up and down the streets of Isla Vista. Whenever we could, we dropped down at low tide to walk the beach. The attention of the dogs was on smells and play; mine was wandering loose and unsure where to anchor itself.

Before too long I got a job that gave me the minimal financial stability I required to begin climbing out of this hole and back in the direction of mainstream society. It was a minimum wage job in a factory. I had landed it because the daughter of the owner did transcendental meditation and I was able to have an interesting conversation with her about spiritual practices. I began immediately.

My workstation at the factory had a window I could gaze out of while I worked. As I took in the vista offered by the Los Padres Mountains I couldn't help but smile: less than a month ago, I was assistant editor of Ananda Marga's worldwide arts magazine, living at its world headquarters in Denver, participating in guerilla warfare trainings meant to change the world order, and surrounded every day by a beehive of activity intent on the grand task of global transformation.

Now? I had a minimum wage factory job, pressure-cooking Styrofoam containers for silicone breast implants, which would then be sent to doctors willing to surgically alter the appearance of their female patients intent on using their charms to secure their share of the American Dream! Life moves in mysterious ways...

The move back to California and my humbling circumstances gave me plenty of time to ruminate on my next steps. For a while longer, I was unable to break free from the desire to access transcendent experiences similar to the one I had had at age 10. I experimented with the easily available psychotropic substances circulating in the community: LSD, Psilocybin, and Peyote. While these provided me with their share of insights about life, my consumption of them reflected shortcut thinking. Gradually, it became clear that the exhilarating clarity of transcendent moments were distractions from the work of transformation.

To genuinely transform I needed to do two things: 1) Solidify my own identity further, and 2) Find a way to honor my desire for self-knowledge without hitching it to a converting organization. Both made me nervous. Who was I outside of the spiritual persona I had so intensely adopted over the last two years? Would I find others willing to pursue self-knowledge without descending into dogma? My final concern was perhaps the most worrying, because it hadn't even been on my radar when I had first joined Ananda Marga: How could I find a way to sound the alarm about a frightening trend I was seeing in society – the co-optation by secular organizations of the conversion strategies perfected by religious groups to more effectively spread their ideologies?

I didn't know the answers to any of these questions, and my emerging confidence was on shaky ground. Nonetheless, it was clear the time had come to break free of ideological systems, and to follow my own instincts about self-knowledge.

21   Krsnamurti, p. 1
22   Storr, p. 192.
23   James, p.
24   Wilber, p. 5
25   Storr, p. 189
26   James, p. 29.

Chapter 6

What Do You Stand For?

> *The point is that we are all capable of believing things which we know to be untrue, and then, when we are finally proved wrong, impudently twisting the facts so as to show that we were right. Intellectually, it is possible to carry on this process for an indefinite time: the only check on it is that sooner or later a false belief bumps up against solid reality, usually on a battlefield.*
>
> *- George Orwell*

When the excitement and intensity of the political, cultural and consciousness explorations of the 60s and 70s gave way to the 80s, I and many others watched as the American corporate world reenergized itself and began to ride the next ideological wave of American society: the pursuit of wealth through free market capitalism. This retooled and much more ideological version of 50s materialism traveled at a pace that kept accelerating, sweeping up society with its grand promise of universal prosperity. My intersections with this wave came through work in the corporate world. In this new environment it was impossible not to notice the parallels between the swoons emanating from corporate board rooms and those I'd previously witnessed in a spiritual context. The inventiveness mixed with snake oil; the arrogant spawning of strategies intended to undermine laws and regulations; the strange combination of organizational management criticizing workers for their shortcomings while simultaneously encouraging them to think of opportunity as endless. This approach was consistent with the principles at the core of the Protestant Reformation and Frontier meta-narratives.

As I watched the meta-narratives and conversion dynamics play out in this wing-tipped manner, I realized how easy it had been to overlook the encroachment of ideology into the freewheeling consciousness experiments of the 60s and 70s. Those experiments had raised expectations to unrealistic and, frequently, utopian levels. This gravitation towards final solutions exposed how easily people with an open-ended attraction to exploring the mysteries of life could be corralled by the structural allure of a perfect society. The deeper this utopian fascination established itself, the more the experimental attitude of the times detoured toward psychological need, surrogate community and compliance with narrowed down interpretations of the dominant meta-narratives. An initial spirit of exuberant exploration had slowly, then furiously, funneled itself into a competition for the best grand theory: one that could provide ultimate answers. This occurred, in part, because the intensity people experienced in their explorations convinced them that adrenal-based emotional excitation was equivalent to transformation. There were certainly exceptions to these detours, but the prevailing zeitgeist had shifted from an environment dominated by creativity and curiosity into one characterized by attempts to "organize" mystery, to capture it inside a perfect belief system. Was this just the way things always worked? Do people creatively seeking self-knowledge always eventually capitulate to authorities promising a paint-by-numbers life? Why had I expected something different?

My heightened expectations had been prompted by the authenticity and ethical rigor characterizing the dramatic social changes taking place in American society during the 50s, 60s and early 70s. Those changes had given substance to hope; the political movements they had spawned had, among other things, changed discriminatory laws and stopped an unjust war. A number of those people, myself included, had come to the conclusion that the spiritual explorations following this political change would simply add to this mix in constructive ways.

By the time I departed Ananda Marga in 1975, however, exactly the opposite seemed to be happening. The society-tipping forces now in play were headed in the opposite direction. Ideological machinery was establishing itself deeper and deeper in both religious and secular organizations. The forces outlined in this book were successfully sabotaging what had begun as an enthusiastic and energetic exploration of consciousness. The genuine urge for self-knowledge was increasingly being replaced by shadow representations of that urge. These shadows looked like the real thing but were tethered to power, to image, and to influence. They were sustained by the support they received from their membership: people who, like myself, steered their direct experience towards ideological security. By doing this, the prospects of finding a grand theory explaining everything could be endlessly entertained - but the ordinariness, uncertainty, and messiness that is central to the transformative process was relegated to the sidelines. The deftness – and aggressiveness – of this marginalization was accelerated by the hyper drive tool bag now being deployed by the marketing and advertising industry. Their never-ending images of perfect beauty, unfaltering strength, easy wealth and endless opportunity aligned seamlessly with the meta-narratives, proceeding from there to assail the senses through the breathtaking advances they had made in their methods of persuasion. All of this was happening at a stunning pace, and the heights of unreality these industries were foisting on society made the task of staying real a challenge for everybody.

With ideologies redirecting the impulse for self-knowledge toward their own ends, a different kind of social change from the one I had imagined was taking root. Organizations were focusing on manufacturing urgency, self-importance, and ultimately identity: identity that conformed to whatever ideology they were pushing. If this trend continued to gain traction, society would end up more conformist, its curiosity crippled, plagued by the boredom that always accompanies pursuit of the superficial - no matter how many "extreme" things people did to prop up a false sense of individuality. Sincere efforts to acquire self-knowledge would continue to be side tracked into the identity hopping process characterizing narcissistic injury. A person might be able to find islands of stability away from mainstream influence and nourish himself with whatever genuine community he discovered, but the difficulty of doing so would challenge the resolve and clarity such a task demanded. Failure would mean being swept under by the almost constant barrage of messages intended to wear down its audience and foster the passivity essential to abandoning personal sovereignty in favor of the latest body of expert knowledge.

This grim scenario frightened me. I was particularly concerned about the growth of psychological passivity I saw all around me. Attributing this passivity to naiveté, a bad childhood or even to a slick, persuasive influence campaign may have been accurate, but it was also insufficient. These were all subcategories of the common thread of identity. Identity was striking me, once again, as the cornerstone of any successful effort a person must make if he wishes to shift himself outside the system and function autonomously. Identity formation had been detoured psychologically by the normalization of narcissism, sociologically through surrogate families, and culturally through unconscious adherence to the meta-narratives. Intensity of feeling through structured ritual could falsely supercharge identity formation on all these levels, deceiving a person into embracing an ephemeral sense of realness and believing it to be the real McCoy. The persuasion factors misdirecting a person gained traction whenever a person did not have a secure adult identity. The more abstract - and distracted - society became, the more difficult it was to provide the right environments for identity to emerge.

Turning around this trend means turning around patterns that are deeply internalized. It means navigating into – rather than away from – everyday environments. Doing so in an aware way links the work of discovering personal identity to its wider context: marriage, raising a family, dealing with the death of loved ones, sickness, friendship, work, community engagement and finding ways to skillfully but genuinely deal with unpredictable circumstances. These ordinary circumstances, which confront all members of the human community, are the grist for the mill of transformation. Addressing them in a real, interconnected, openhearted way is the work required. The difficulty with this is that because ordinary living is so much grittier than the pursuit of transcendent experiences, and because a solid identity is the exception rather than the rule in society, this work can be easily redirected by emotionally exciting rituals promising an easier and quicker path to fame, fortune, or a slice of paradise. The importance of the ordinary has been trampled by ideological tsunamis of infinite variety offering patented solutions which depend on the normalization of narcissism, and which emphasize impression management versus immersion in the real. Navigating through day-to-day life skillfully requires a blend of inner receptivity, humility, generosity, ethical awareness, deepening self-trust, connection to community and a willingness to act invisibly much of the time. These are not qualities mainstream society currently encourages.

Ideologies use the normalization of narcissism as the scaffolding for their seemingly straightforward alternative: a ready-made identity, a family of like-minded people, and the seductions of a final solution. These things move a person further and further from anything real. They invite him to live in a world of mental fantasy, shielded from responsibility, engaged increasingly in bubble realities. This encourages a 'strange blend of passive consumption mixed with endless activity so characteristic of what's currently deemed a normal life. Productivity, achievement, and success are benchmarks set for him rather than by him. This is a far cry from what genuine success looks like: building something in the world that flows from a person's own dreamings, and which contributes to a larger sense of community.

My own determination to remain vigilant about relinquishing my sovereignty to an ideology required acting in ways that were less and less susceptible to being hijacked by trance states. What did this mean now, 35 years after my fundamentalist detour? What did it mean in a global environment, where the damaging impact of ideological decisions is magnified by the ever-increasing interconnectedness of the world community? The challenge now was to conduct the search for self-knowledge in a world whose limits were becoming as obvious as its frontiers had formerly been.

Successfully coming to terms with limits is one of the main indicators that a person has moved from a malfunctioning narcissism to healthy self-confidence. Can he handle the frustration that comes with recognizing that the world out there is not structured solely to satisfy his personal needs? Only then will he begin to appreciate what limits are really about, and what respecting the surrounding context means.

Grasping this lesson is not just a matter of altering a personal sense of entitlement. It's a commitment to changing the mindset of limitless expectations fostered by the frontier meta-narrative. It's the cultivation of the self-compassion necessary to stand down from puritanical notions of perfection. It's the effort involved in building communities that are inclusive of everyone. Doing these things strengthens a person's capacity to keep ideologies at bay. If a person's identity is solid and broadly contextualized, he'll have enough depth and confidence to take in exhilaration, hope, and inspiration without forgetting to do so with the proverbial grain of salt. The visions of equality put forward by the civil rights movement in the 50s, the push for peace in the 60s, and the advocacy of social inclusion and mutual respect in the 70s were hugely important turning points for society. The challenges each of them presented, however, was one of perspective: to be moved by them without entering into the trance states any set of inspirational ideas can invoke.

What had characterized the identity of people inside these movements who had kept their head level in spite of all the noise around them? It appeared as though they had done something very simple: they had viewed the seminal ideas of their movements simply as *starting points*. Starting points reminding them of the possibility of living a useful, fulfilling human life while remaining connected to others doing the same. Starting points in the same way my mystical experience could have been viewed, had I been able to do so at the time - a glimpse into the possible, not the ultimate.

The equanimity this requires recognizes that inspiration of any sort is a double-edged sword. On the one hand being inspired results in a sense of expansiveness and creativity. On the other hand, the seduction of its promise can easily overtake and befuddle a less than solid identity. Whenever a person over-identifies with any external motivation, he quickly loses track of any guidance from his inner compass. The evidence I had of this in my own life included times when I had allowed inspiration to prompt me to be evangelical to others; or when I had cut ethical corners because of my certainty about what I deemed was right for everyone; or when I had cut off empathy in order to stay "focused." These actions seemed insignificant at the time, but all of them indicated I had lost track of the need to weigh the information I was receiving against something reliable inside myself. When that went missing, my initiative became disconnected from my capacity to reflect more widely on the broader context. This included curtailing the ongoing receptivity I needed to hear corrective feedback about my actions.

Without a solid identity as a base, polarities such as receptivity and initiative become homogenized. The anxieties presented by considering when to act and when to listen, how the wider context affects the situation, and other complexities are avoided. A person then digs mental foxholes inside his overly simplified worldview, cutting off any feedback not supportive of his ideology, and working furiously to foist that ideology onto non-believers. He uses any inspiration he encounters to reinforce the notion of a final solution to complex problems, rather than as starting points requiring a lot of work with others to get right. Inspiration becomes one of the quickest ways to whisk a person seeking identity further into the arms of ideology.

The shield of exuberance provided by inspiration allows ideologies to function as wolves in sheep's clothing. Powerful ideas, often groundbreaking, get packaged into seemingly supportive organizational structures and sold as universal truths. They wrap themselves in a certainty that instantly appeals to both the angels and demons of human nature. The angels seek inspiration in order to take action that is visionary and contributory. The demons want inspiration as a means of satisfying unmet needs. The latter have a ravenous and unending appetitiveness, and can easily overturn the good intentions of the former. This will invariably happen unless a strong identity and wide-ranging, authentic relationships are in place that can redirect this process towards something grounded and genuine.

One of the most compelling psychological needs driving an inspired person whose identity is wobbly is the desire for predictability and order. This desire is a substitute for the solid sense of self gained when identity is discovered through an emergent rather than adopted process. It made me wonder how the desire for order and predictability, which everyone has to some degree, could be fulfilled without ideology. Could this happen in a way that didn't compromise a sense of respect for things unknowable? What would allow people to have a deeper sense of trust about their surroundings, to fend off ideological promises of certainty? What would it take to cultivate trust in the notion that some things must always remain mysterious - and that our role as humans is not always to solve mysteries, but to enter into them more deeply? James Carse, in his book *The Religious Case Against Belief*, makes a convincing argument that this, rather than proclaiming absolute notions of truth, is the genuine purpose of religion, and is responsible for its institutional endurance over centuries.

I had already concluded that one way to trust more in life's inherent mysteries was to not let the excitement of powerful, direct experiences propel me into imaginative inflation. The fact that inspirational moments highlight humanity's greatest capacities – the ability to dream, to create powerful images of mystery, or to contemplate extraordinary improvements in society – can result in an "accordion" effect: it can instantly blow up an idea to extraordinary dimensions, then squeeze it back into its box in a frantic desire to possess it. Both of these impulses run contrary to simply letting the idea flow forward, and finding a way to add something to it along the way. The second stage of the accordion effect is particularly devastating because when dreaming is contracted into the lifeless machinery of ideology, the mystery and curiosity that initially attracts people gets replaced by emotional excitation, and the desire to recreate it. What does it take to continue to trust ongoing direct experience when the gold rush for some sort of final "truth" is surging out of every corner of society? To stay in the moment instead of jumping into endless explanations of it?

> The fundamental understanding of oneself does not come through knowledge or through the accumulation of experiences, which is merely the cultivation of memory. The understanding of oneself is from moment to moment; if we merely accumulate knowledge of the self, that very knowledge prevents further understanding, because accumulated knowledge and experience become the center through which thought focuses and has its being.[27]

This Krsnamurti quote confirms something many people have discovered: sustaining mindful presence provides all the self-knowledge a person needs. It's not just memory, knowledge and experience that people use to avoid being in the present moment, however. It's the beliefs a person has.

Everyone has beliefs about lots of different things, and it's not an indication that a person is bounded by ideology when this is the case. Proponents of ideologies have learned how to steer strong beliefs to their advantage, however, through the mechanisms discussed in this book. As a result, comprehensively organized, intractable beliefs lie at the core of every ideology. They are there for a good reason: they offer extraordinary benefits to a person. The first of these benefits is the way beliefs take a person out of an everyday reality fraught with anxiety, suffering, and the problems of the world. Escape from this feels good. Belief provides escape through the reassurance and refuge it offers.

This good feeling is enhanced by a second benefit: the new reality a person inhabits when he embraces belief makes him more capable than he otherwise would be to accomplish seemingly impossible things: including things in that first, ordinary reality. It doesn't matter if this strength is adversarial or fear based, as explored in the previous chapter. That doesn't minimize the enormity of what gets accomplished in the world: quite the contrary. When a person's accomplishments are credited to external sources he inflates his adopted identity, taking him further from the reality of a situation. His success gets tethered to the surrogate community he has joined, and his adopted identity takes heart. He ends up conducting his life in ways that are both irrational and fearless, because he knows that if things don't work out he has a belief system and an ideological family to fall back on.

In the 1950s, a Minneapolis woman, known pseudonymously as Marian Keech, believed herself to be in communication with alien beings through automatic writing. These alien beings had told her a great flood would cleanse the world on December 21, 1954. She and others who believed her were confident they would be saved from this catastrophe by extraterrestrials that would take them to safety in their spacecraft just before the event. When this failed to happen, what was their response? Was it a weakening of belief?

No, quite the opposite. Their belief became stronger. They proclaimed that the prayers they had made to prevent the catastrophe must have worked to save the planet. This incredible capacity for belief to hijack reason has countless examples similar to this very well known one. Sometimes, those examples produce outcomes that inspire us all, such as people recovering from diseases after medical authorities have declared it impossible to do so. The important thing to recognize about strong belief is that it gives a person both relief from suffering and empowerment. Is it any wonder why ideologies, constructed on a foundation of carefully interwoven beliefs, are so attractive?

The unquestionable power and allure of belief is why it's impossible, and undesirable, to structure a life without keeping beliefs somewhere in the picture. The problem, given how easily beliefs destroy lives when they calcify into ideology, is coming to terms with where and how they should fit into human affairs. This may be the most important conundrum facing human society at the moment. It is certainly one of the most confronting.

What was my personal response to this challenge going to be? How could I accept the power, usefulness, and centrality of beliefs to human life, yet de-link them from all the constraints of ideology I had discovered? Was this even possible? I was confronted by the seemingly airtight weave between ideology and beliefs, but creating space between them seemed central to discovering new ways to pursue self-knowledge.

My experience with Ananda Marga had fueled this desire to distinguish between the extraordinary things beliefs can lead to and the incredible damage they can wreak.

The beginning of my curiosity about this issue had come, surprisingly, during a very small incident that occurred during those years. It was a time when I was a passenger in a van with a Buddhist driver. He had a mosquito on his arm, and because of his belief in non-harm, he was trying to gently shoo it out the window. In the process of focusing on getting the mosquito out the window, he ran over a rabbit crossing the road! Beliefs are like that: they give a person focus and conviction, but they narrow his perspective of the wider world. Sometimes this narrowing of focus is greatly needed to move him into action. Sometimes, however, that narrowness leads him to do the exact opposite of his stated intention. Beliefs are supreme motivators, capable of pushing aside doubt and generating enthusiasm about practically anything. In doing so, however, they block a more panoramic access to the present moment.

When living in the world is based exclusively on belief, all the obstacles associated with narrowness of thought and the rigidity of unbending conviction block alternative ways forward. Narrowness and rigidity work against a wider awareness of the world and creative interaction with it. As John Ralston Saul has written, "The best way to control imagination is to insist on belief."[28] Extreme belief squeezes creativity out of a person's life and replaces it with certainty. He then views the world around him through a rigid ideological lens, a world populated by shadow realities. Once he makes that leap, knowingly or unknowingly, he will stop basing his actions on direct experience, curiosity, or experimentation. Instead, he will determine what to do by filtering events in the world through particular ideas about how things are supposed to be. Those ideas may or may not be relevant to circumstances he is experiencing in the moment.

All of this occurs largely because a critical dimension of belief serves to wrap a person in a false identity and keep him there. That dimension is the emotionality of belief. It is a factor that is never far from the surface of any true believer. This interrelationship between belief and emotion frequently perplexed me when I was at the deepest point of immersion in my Ananda Marga conversion swoon. Convincing bits of the ideology delivered by a charismatic, articulate person were capable of shaping my understanding by playing on my emotions. Emotions provided the intensity necessary to steer my perceptions away from a process based on self-discovery and towards one based on the ideas of others.

How do emotions and belief intersect, and affect the conversion process? How do they detour identity away from something discovered and towards something someone else would like a person to be?

Jean Paul Sartre spent considerable time examining the connection between emotions and belief. He considered emotions to be a primary way most people have of apprehending the world. He added the idea that the physiological dimension of emotions is what gives them a sense of realness, because a person lives emotions in his body and in the world. Emotions can thus seemingly transform the world into something magical. A belief in magic gives a person the opportunity to avoid the work of real transformation, while simultaneously feeling he is doing exactly that. Reinforcing a belief in magic is the task of emotion. Or, as Sartre himself puts it:

> "We can now conceive what an emotion is. It is a transformation of the world. When the paths before us become too difficult, or when we cannot see our way, we can no longer put up with such an exacting and difficult world. All ways are barred and nevertheless we must act. So then we try to change the world; that is, to live it as though the relations between things and their potentialities were not governed by deterministic processes but by magic. But, be it well understood, this is no playful matter: we are cornered, and we fling ourselves into this new attitude with all the force at our command. Note also that our effort is not conscious of what it is, for then it would be an object of reflection."[29]

The transformation Sartre is referring to is not the kind that leads to greater self-knowledge. It is the kind that leads to greater certainty wrapped in emotionality, which heightens a false sense of realness. It's easy to view emotionality and realness synonymously; the sense of aliveness the former brings serves as a stark contrast to the life of everyday routine that entraps most people. The forcefulness of that emotionality provides a temporary jolt that can override not just reason but the broader awareness of a person. The internal struggles I experienced when deciding whether something in Ananda Marga philosophy was consistent with my experience of the world were frequently characterized by emotionality functioning in this way. This was particularly the case when the realities of the organization ran contrary to beliefs I held before joining it.

One belief I had before Ananda Marga was in the value of collaborative, democratic ways of making decisions. I had trained in ways to ensure this happened in therapy groups, self-development classes, and other contexts I worked in where I had influence. If I still supported this idea, why had I joined a "guru-centric" organization that was not only extremely hierarchical but which bore a much closer structural resemblance to totalitarianism than it did to democracy?

My emotions clanged against each other furiously as I pitted old beliefs such as this one against the new ones I sought to assimilate. My desire to embrace Ananda Marga ideology had grown strong enough that I threw my will behind its philosophy in a way that would have made Marion Keech proud. The most common strategy I employed in my inner battlefield is the one everyone uses to deal with cognitive dissonance: I pushed the information out of awareness altogether. How different is this process from a person putting his faith so completely in free market ideology that he buys a house three times more expensive than he can afford because he's convinced markets will "always go up"? Or who thumbs his nose at the scientific research validating the impact of human activity on climate and continues to live as if resources are infinite?

When I was at the height of my own cognitive dissonance, I built up an incredible amount of tension inside my own psyche. Cognitive dissonance theory[30] states that once dissonance reaches this "almost-intolerable" level, a person will actively avoid situations that increase the dissonance. For me that meant moving my identity deeper and deeper into the one Ananda Marga was providing for me. The refuge it offered, the empowerment it provided, eased the dissonance. Where will the people ignoring economic, environmental and other contemporary realities take refuge? What will they do to feel empowered?

This tension between emotions and clear thinking is a product of the way human beings process decisions connected to beliefs. When a person chooses a particular belief, or belief system, to be the anchor for his decisions, it allows him to take action in the world that carries with it a sense of meaning. That meaning, even if it's not yet funneled through an ideology, will invariably have links to an underlying meta-narrative, providing an additional layer of psychological security. This quickly resolves internal debates such as those I've described in previous chapters, debates that can paralyze a person's ability to take action. Paralysis and doubt are states of mind most people avoid like the plague. Deciding something – anything – is usually seen as preferable to either.

Standing behind a belief also reflects the desire a person has to understand direct experience after the fact of its occurrence, to make sense of it. It frames the experience, provides a sense of solidity, and this makes future actions easier to take. As a result, all of us do it. The consequence of this, however, is to take a person from the present moment into something abstract. Given that staying present is one of the hardest tasks a human being can undertake, it's understandable that such refuge would occasionally be sought. The danger lies in doing so unconsciously, and closing the door on the benefits doubt can bring: open-mindedness, creativity, and a willingness to view the wider context.

How often does a person trust himself to meet the world in a direct, unfiltered manner without taking excessive refuge in belief? To endure the anxieties produced by doubt without losing track of himself? My own experience led me to conclude that people capable of doing this with any sort of consistency are extremely rare. It is much more common for beliefs to intervene, consciously or unconsciously, between direct experience and action. For example, when I considered my life long opposition to violence, I could see it was a belief that I had formed long ago as a result of direct experience. Did that mean there was now no place for violence, ever? To conclude this would be to take refuge in my belief. Would I feel this way if the lives of my children were under threat and addressing that threat successfully was only possible through violence? Would my belief provide a fatal hesitation? The challenge in situations such as these is enormous: stay in the present, remain open to past experience, and don't allow belief to push aside the information a current situation puts forward. In other words, don't try to live without beliefs. Instead, develop the awareness and identity necessary to put them to the side and change them if experience suggests it would be right to do so. Determining what is "right" in a situation requires a finely tuned inner compass connected to a solid sense of self and, even then, mistakes will be made.

Of course, the pressure to act in the world – and increasingly in today's world, to act quickly – means that every person is susceptible to the chaos of warring belief systems and all the persuasion they carry at moments of paralysis and doubt. Because a person in such situations wants, more than anything, to relieve pressure, he will usually determine that this is most easily accomplished by making decisions based on belief. Exercising the power of presence needed to fully "drop into" the situation is much more challenging, and the sense of timelessness required to do so runs contrary to the clock driven realities most people yield to in life. It's not that it's impossible to drop into situations quickly. It's just that this is much more likely to happen when a person has a solid identity. Acting from belief is much easier, even when a person knows that doing so can block a larger awareness. Acting from belief means a person's adopted identity can be protected by emotion with varying degrees of fierceness, depending on how closely aligned that belief is to his identity.

The power of this will be grasped by anyone who thinks about the emotional heat generated by himself and others during combative moments with each other. When that heat is extreme, it becomes close to impossible to question any opinions stated by the other person in the throes of that emotion. It is equally difficult to take in the contrary opinions that person is expressing. Each person's identity, the role it stems from, and the beliefs at its foundation are all under the protection of emotion. This whole process runs counter to being truly present, and to the courage required to break emotional logjams. In other words, when identity constructed upon belief is bolted into place with emotion, the biggest and first casualty is awareness. Opportunities to transform are overridden. In their place, a person looks for opportunities to confirm his beliefs. Depth of thinking and clarity disappear from the landscape.

Suspending belief requires the discipline of keeping the mind open and attending to the surrounding world with panoramic mindfulness until emotional heat subsides and other factors can become involved: factors such as reason, memory, courage, and an ethical sense. These factors don't preclude the eventual formation of a belief, they simply prevent its premature arrival and any inflated position a person may subsequently give to that belief. If action can emanate from these things in concert with direct experience of the world, rather than from emotional impulse and/or ideas about the world, a person moves into the present. Easier said than done.

Does this mean emotions have no constructive place in a human life? No. The phenomenologist Pradine echoed Sartres when he commented on the power of emotion and its enormous capacity to distort perception. He did not discount feeling states altogether, however. Instead, he made a distinction between *sentiment* and emotion. His definition of sentiments was that they are complex and valuable feelings associated with perception, whereas emotions are the way sentiments become extreme and disorganized.

> "Emotions...reduce sentiments almost to reflex; they are sentiments in the extreme, explosive, crises form...
> Sentiments and emotions come from the imagination, one being adaptive and the other maladaptive. Emotional reactions tend to squash the more gentle and adaptive sentiments. Emotion is a mental and motor disaster experienced by the subject who is its victim."[31]

The manner in which strong emotions overpower sentiments becomes clearer when considering three differences between emergent identity and adopted identity, and how much more susceptible to disorienting emotions the latter is:

1). A person who allows his identity to emerge has access to deeper, transpersonal wisdom which can shape his life and direct him toward the transformation he needs to make. Anyone who allows his identity to emerge is more capable of noticing the deeper, interior currents calling him to a larger sense of self. For a person who trusts emergent identity, that relationship is a strong one. It also prompts a person to develop the ability to quiet emotion enough to be able to access these callings.

2). A person who allows his identity to emerge recognizes that no act of transformation is a "final step." It is just the best step at the time, one that expands horizons – but horizons that will themselves need to be exceeded in the future. Enough solidity has to be mustered to make this leap while simultaneously knowing that "all the answers to everything" will not be what is achieved. Great uncertainty exists about what the outcome of such change will be; a marked distinction from the ideological narratives provided after the manufacture of predictable miracles in fundamentalist environments. Tolerating that uncertainty and being willing to resist any notions of a final step demand a mature level of emotional intelligence.

3). If a person allows his identity to emerge, he will manage the existential fear that accompanies *identity shedding* more skillfully, and with less susceptibility to conversion. There are two reasons for this. The first is that the experience of having trusted the emergence of identity before means a person is less likely to try on someone else's prescribed personality when he sheds an identity in order to transform his life. He will be more willing to tolerate the uncertainty this change brings because he appreciates that something new and more aware is on its way. Furthermore, he will know from experience that dropping an identity does not mean his core sense of "I-ness" will disappear. That gives him the necessary ballast to navigate through the liberation he will feel from dropping the old identity, and which make him vulnerable to an urgency to "fill up" the empty space. His experience with emergent identity will have taught him that finding a way through existential vulnerability is the only way to end up with something authentic: something of his own.

Of these three differences, the third one is the most challenging because it involves fear. Fear has the greatest capacity of any emotion to immobilize a human being. As children, that fear is primal when identity is first being formed: it's the fear of critical caregiver relationships disappearing if the desired identity isn't adopted; it's the fear of whether one can survive without that caregiver support. These extraordinarily powerful fears, coupled with the shame a child experiences when he acts in ways that displease his caregivers, are capable of thwarting a person's successful navigation through the narcissistic phase of identity development. The impact of fear on clarity and courage is so debilitating that unless a person has accidentally or intentionally bumped up against some sense of real identity inside himself, he will never even consider standing up against the false ones always being offered to him: initially by caregivers, and then from influences he embraces at crucial points later in life. Doing so requires emotional courage.

Not doing so makes a person vulnerable to conversion in matters large and small, usually without his even knowing that's the case. The lack of the experience of emergent identity causes him to be dismissive of any warnings issued about the dangers of allowing ideologues, even blatant ones living in the world as fundamentalists, a license to act on his behalf, especially if he unconsciously senses he might gain a sense of identity through compliance to their directives. Fear prompts him to turn to the false hopes such groups provide as a predictable pathway to inner security. This false hope depends on the person concluding that belief is the antidote to fear.

Allowing identity to emerge means facing fear head on and seeking the greater awareness it brings. It requires risk-taking, vulnerability, active curiosity, and the capacity to endure doubt – not certainty and control. It is a lifelong endeavor, one in which identities previously assumed are deconstructed, so that a person can step into something that reflects a deeper current, something which honors the gifts he has and the contributions he can make to the world. Change of this sort is gradual, punctuated with occasional breakthroughs which, if genuine, reflect previously laid groundwork. Genuine identity is not a matter of adopting someone else's quick fix prescriptions. It is a matter of discovering one's self over time.

How far does this push belief out of the picture? What about the powerful positive impact it can have on human life?

This particular question caused as much confusion as any I considered after my departure from Ananda Marga. I desperately wanted to establish my life in direct experience to avoid the pitfalls of conversion I had experienced. The isolation of not operating ideologically, however, made life feel as though it was perpetually in limbo. Everywhere I went, people were throwing their lives into systems of belief, diving in head first in ways that infused them with emotionalized excitement, however temporary this ultimately proved to be. In contrast, the spiritual path I saw in front of me looked more like a Sisyphean task devoid of the inspiration and the boldness strong belief brings forth. Was there an answer to this? Was there a way to still be empowered by belief without being a slave to it?

The more I climbed into my ordinary life, the clearer the answer to this question became: *No, there isn't one - at least not inside of any ideological system.* No final workshop providing all the necessary foundational beliefs. No stunning theory of everything closing all the loopholes of doubt. No compelling map charting every inlet or listing every contour with exactitude. What there is are the starting points, and the work that follows them.

Ironically, understanding both the power and the limitations of inspiration – and the starting points it reveals – led me to discover the role of belief in my life. I realized that if the same openness that offers awareness of starting points can be sustained through presence of mind, the real work of transformation and self-knowledge could be done. Moving from inspiration to sustaining presence of mind is facilitated if a person believes that life's ongoing uncertainty is something to be embraced, rather than seen as a handicap. Believing this means that the seemingly infinite capacity for paradox life puts in front of a person, or the multitude of ways it keeps throwing him back upon himself, are challenges to get real. They are invitations to recognize that the same approach used to navigate through any difficult situation will rarely work in precisely the same manner for other situations, no matter how similar those situations may appear to be to each other.

The importance of learning to embrace uncertainty – learning to believe in it – became evident to me through a series of both joyous and tragic life events. The birth of my children. The suicide death of my wife, four years after our divorce. Immigration to one country, then another.

All these events brought the mirror closer. Humbling and seemingly continuous revelations of how short I fell of the absolutist standards I had set for myself in life, and then the yielding of my embarrassment to an acceptance of the inevitability of mistake-making and the surety of its presence the rest of my days.

Out of all this, my desire to live with belief found a home in the process of life itself. This allowed me to make some distinctions. The first was between the magical thinking I described earlier, and the ultimately unfathomable mystery of life. The latter, through awe, provides all the sense of genuine magic a person could desire. This is a well that never runs dry if a person's curiosity and intention to learn is nourished. Since none of us can even come close to learning all the life knowledge he desires, living skillfully means believing life will inevitably supply a person with the circumstances he needs to learn the most important things: the bits that allow him to address whatever challenges he is equipped, or almost equipped, to face. The job begins by keeping eyes, mind, and heart open enough to notice the flagging tape. It gains traction when that awareness is sustained. All of this demanded I take on a second belief: in awareness itself. Awareness accompanies all self-discovered identity change, and increasing awareness is the primary work required to advance self-knowledge. Awareness that results from a continual process of allowing identity to emerge, not from adopting it to lay over narcissistic injury.

Beliefs are similar to the railings on a swing bridge running across a dangerous gorge. They are an integral part of the structure that helps to carry a person forward, but no more important than the support frames bolted into the gorge walls, the planks he has to walk on, or the soundness of the bridge's design. The various dimensions of being human that can complement belief need to be there: building a solid identity, relating to others authentically, and being willing to meet the world in the present moment. When a person adopts identity, however, the entire swing bridge is made of beliefs. He identifies with them so thoroughly that he turns away from the work required to become a more aware human being.

This is what happens in fundamentalist environments, and it leads to a person fearing rather than respecting his own vulnerability. He fails to recognize the possibilities vulnerability offers to a more panoramic awareness and to an expanded, stronger identity. When vulnerability is feared in this way, it has numerous implications. One of the most important of these is the way the growth of a person's ethical sense gets stunted. When an ideological system crosses the line into fundamentalism, it becomes totalitarian in all respects: it views the rest of humanity as composed of people to either convert or to defeat.

There is no acceptance of difference, or appreciation for ideas operating outside the orbit of the ideology's viewpoint. This pushes everyone inside the system towards conformity. More importantly, it reduces ethical decision-making, which requires navigating through complexity, to the level of moral dictates, which prescribe uniform ways to act. The sole purpose at the core of an ideology's moral dictates is to guide behavior to conform to its objectives.

The depth and nuance required to respond ethically in complex situations, on the other hand, throws a person back on his identity. Ethical dilemmas are the toughest of all testing grounds for whatever is operating as a sense of self inside a person. Navigating through these dilemmas successfully demands a strong sense of identity: knowing where that sense of self stands, how far to trust it, and when to reach out for something new. It requires having the awareness that while there are dimensions of ethical situations that will be unknown, it is critical not to allow that lack of knowing to inhibit the courage necessary to act if necessary.

It also means being able to discriminate between embracing a different perspective because it will lead to an appropriate ethical resolution versus embracing a different perspective because it reduces the uncertainty of that situation. The way through an ethical dilemma often requires yielding to something unfamiliar, something that may run contrary to a dearly held belief. Provided the decision to act is not impulsive, it will be based on an internal sense of rightness. Is that sense of rightness a mixture of experience, imagination, compassion, presence of mind, intelligence, common sense and the other qualities that characterize a solid identity? If so, the person will be able to tolerate an ongoing sense of uncertainty as the ethical situation unfolds. If, however, that sense of rightness is more "feeling-based," i.e. geared toward jumping away from the problem or from wanting to wave it out of the way, then it is the act of a less-than-solid identity seeking comfort. This is a point of identity vulnerability. Decisions stemming from an impatient desire to be rid of a problem indicate a person's fearful relationship to vulnerability. This increases his susceptibility to ideas offered by charismatic, articulate spokespeople of an ideology, a susceptibility that has ramifications beyond the immediate ethical dilemma a person may be facing. His acquiescence is not just to the solution offered by an external authority; it is an agreement to allow his identity to be shaped by that authority.

One way to begin navigating through territory such as this is to recognize that what an ideologue offers to a complex ethical situation will always be some form of certainty. Grasping at that certainty because it reduces existential anxiety is different from embracing it because a sense of rightness is perceived. Doing the latter does not remove doubt. It coexists with it, allowing for movement to be made but demanding that awareness be sustained if an appropriate resolution is to be secured. Ethical explorations are facilitated when those involved in making them are conscious of respecting the ideas of all concerned, including those opposite to their own. If a person can offer awareness and presence in the midst of contrary ideas, this usually signals his understanding that any declarations of premature certainty interrupt a process which might lead to ethical clarity.

This same capacity to resist a rush to certainty is a powerful tool to employ for anyone who is supporting a person when he is transforming his identity. The direction in which the person's new identity will lead can be guessed at but is never fully known in advance. If the person who is transforming his identity is fortunate enough to be in the presence of someone who offers respectful support while he is identity shedding, the first person's own appreciation of the mysterious dimension of life, and of the way interconnectedness can support that, will deepen. The fact that people outside of one's self exist who are capable and willing to provide helpful contact during such a major transition is one of the most uplifting, hopeful dimensions of the human experience. It awakens a person's sense of interconnectedness because he realizes that self-knowledge depends not just on self-generated acts of will, not just on providence, but on the helping hands that appear, often out of nowhere, from other people along the way. Those helping hands may not necessarily come from the well of like-mindedness. This is a powerful inducement for the recipient of such support to take more responsibility for his actions, which is central not only to establishing his new identity but to acting ethically in the future. In other words, he will better equipped to travel through the rugged territory of both personal transformation and ethical dilemmas.

Examples of how ethical concerns don't get addressed well in ideological organizations abound, and highlight how different the responses of people accustomed to adopting identity are to those who are committed to discovering it. The most obvious of these are the ethical concerns raised by the process of conversion itself. Those concerns are not evident initially: at the point where a person conveys his excitement about something he's discovered and wants to share that excitement. That's the most natural thing in the world. It's later in the process when things run aground: at the point where a person ceases to listen to the objections or disinterest of his audience. An ethically grounded person, secure in his own identity, doesn't do this. He becomes skilled at applying the minimal amount of force to any persuasive effort he makes. Just as a caring and aware parent allows his child to self-develop while simultaneously protecting him from dangers he may not see, an ethically grounded person interacts with other adults he wishes to persuade in a manner that is capable of restraint when his excitement threatens to cross the threshold of the other person's autonomy. He interacts with the door still open to the possibility that *his* perspective, not the other person's, might change. Isn't the violation of autonomy precisely the point where belief hijacks not only direct experience, but also the respect necessary for authentic relationship? Isn't the whole act of imposing ideas onto someone else irrespective of that person's response an ethical failing? Doesn't this parallel the process by which an impatient caregiver imposes his preferred identity on his child, rather than encouraging one to emerge? Aren't adopted identities foisted upon children the starting point priming the pump for later susceptibility to conversion of all shapes and sizes? When I considered these questions, it gave me a deeper appreciation for how easily and thoroughly a person's ethical development can be derailed when identity is adopted. The solid sense of self necessary to make tough ethical choices never establishes itself. After my departure from Ananda Marga, I became acutely aware of the link between ethical under development and the likelihood that some form of ideology was operating behind the scenes.

The combination of thinking about these differences in identity formation, the ethical concerns this raised, the fact that a place for belief could exist in my post-ideological life, and the sum of my experiences in Ananda Marga returned my thoughts to how I would pursue self-knowledge once I left the organization. Would this be something I could do with others again? Which of the techniques that I had learned would I continue to use? How would I combine the work of solidifying, then expanding, my identity with the work of accessing life's mysteries in ways unimpeded by trance states?

Before I could attend to these questions, I needed to review the *persuasion continuum* mentioned earlier when this book was exploring the importance of Stanley Milgram's work. That continuum begins with the benign efforts of trying to convince somebody of something relatively insignificant. It ends with the much more serious efforts of fundamentalists intent on structuring every corner of a person's life. *Intensity of experience* and *solidity of identity* are the two factors primarily determining where on this continuum a person falls, and how that shapes the degree to which he will rely on belief rather than his own inner compass. Intensity of experience combined with a shaky identity obviously pushes the needle towards extreme susceptibility to the fundamentalist side of the continuum. A solid identity and the capacity to function largely on self-motivation characterize the other extreme, increasing the likelihood that a person's consideration of external factors will not impede his ability to come to his own conclusions. This seems straightforward enough until it's recognized that an adopted identity based on strong beliefs creates a false impression in a person's mind that his identity is solid. He doesn't discover what a fragile house he's living in until the heat is turned up through some form of emotional excitation. This doesn't have to be through an organized conversion ritual involving large numbers of people. It can happen through a bullying boss at work, a salesman on the phone pushing a product the person doesn't really want, or a dependent family member taking advantage of the person's inability to establish firm boundaries. These and similar challenges are ones people face regularly in their lives; challenges which, if unmet, make a person more susceptible to functioning ideologically. Their ordinariness obscures how important they are in determining where on the persuasion continuum a person might be at a particular point in time. It is through countless small acts of compromise that the construction of a solid identity is undermined. All these small actions soften the soil for ideological susceptibility to take root. The distinctions between persuasion and ideology, between ideology and fundamentalism – between all points on this continuum – are differences of degree, not of kind. Examining the tipping points along the persuasion continuum more closely proved helpful to me in understanding how persuasion intersects with identity and intensity of experience.

The mystical experience I had as a child is an example of how intensity can impact a yet-to-be-fully-formed identity; particularly the way my confusion about it led me towards a desire for ideological certainty. As mentioned previously, when I had this experience, it wasn't just the urge to repeat it that drove my behavior. It was also my urge to understand it. That led me to an attraction to theories that could explain the experience, and to be open to persuasion by advocates of those theories. It's human nature for this to happen whenever a person seeks to understand how something works. Theories, if embraced as temporary scaffolding rather than absolute foundations, are capable of nudging the awareness and knowledge of a person forward. The challenge in doing so successfully, however, requires that a person continually bear in mind that any theory is an *abstraction*. If this is forgotten, the persons runs the risk of becoming so entranced with them that he foregoes staying in the present. That makes him vulnerable to being led astray by the intensity of any experience connected to the theory. As Sartre has said: "Evil is the systematic substitution of the abstract for the concrete."[32]

Embracing theories begins innocently enough when they align with a person's experience. When that happens, he's likely to give the theory some degree of credibility. In doing so, he begins the process of believing in the theory, and steps down the road of abstracting the original experience.

All this defines normal learning processes unless, at some point, unmet personal needs enter the picture and confuse things in some way that brings those needs out of the shadows. This can happen through something as simple as inspiration. When these needs surface embedded in an adopted rather than discovered identity, the person's excitement about what he's experiencing moves him further along the persuasion continuum. It can lead him to calcify the theory he's been considering, turning it into more of a certainty in his mind.

Calcification is the *first tipping point*. When it occurs, a person may start to override direct experience in favor of belief. This doesn't mean he can't trust theories as indicators of how life works. Everybody does that and couldn't function in the world without doing so. The calcification being discussed here is the line that's crossed when that trust overreaches itself; a phenomenon precipitated when the urgency of personal need becomes more salient than a person's inner compass. Calcification means he is less willing to adapt when confronted with contradictory information. It's the point where the door to open-minded consideration of all options first closes. When this happens, he starts to live inside the world of ideas he's embraced. Since everyone has thresholds beyond which tolerating too much ambiguity in life becomes too difficult, everyone engages to some degree in calcification.

Calcification doesn't totally thwart a person's awareness and flexibility. What it does do is initiate an internal battle between beliefs he's adopting and ones he has held previously. The intensity of these internal battles depends on the solidity of identity; particularly how much a person's psychological needs are pressing in on him. If that pressure is intense, calcification will travel further down the persuasion continuum and cross a *second tipping point*: the embrace of ideology. Embracing ideology activates the tendency to deny opposing viewpoints, and sets the stage for a person to trade off bits of his sovereignty. The degree to which he will make that trade depends on whether he determines, correctly or incorrectly, that his personal needs are being addressed. External surrogacy environments, if they exist, become more of a factor at this point. They combine a person's internal process with the building of an elaborate, abstract framework consistent with the ideology's perspective. This prompts him to "practice" filtering experience through the beliefs he's taken on board. His internal battles will still occasionally puncture awareness, however, heightening the importance, for the converting organization, of surrogacy and emotive ritual to sustain his commitment. His belief in the ideology's theories will grow faster if he limits his contact with anyone outside the ideology, and this weakens any initial desire he may have had for verification of the ideology's perspective. At this stage, any doubts he has will likely be assuaged sufficiently by testimonials and the edification he feels from having everyone around him share the beliefs he's adopted.

Testing a theory in the wider world involves more than testimonials. It requires examining the theory's claims to see if they hold up under experimental pressure. Theoretical claims are also a type of calcification, but experiments are meant to determine the extent to which the calcified bits under consideration hold true. Some level of calcification is essential as glue for any theory; it allows a person to act in the world without questioning every detail. Too much glue, however, gums up the works: it closes off considering any exceptions to whatever the theory is attempting to explain. This is the point at which ideologies diverge from theory.

The test for determining when calcification has led to ideological rigidity appears whenever something new comes along which disproves some aspect of the ideology: i.e. Marion Keech's aliens don't show up. If calcification has advanced enough, a person whose views are based on hardened ideas will have abandoned the capacity to appreciate the merit of a new idea; he will have become an ideologue. In extreme cases, he won't even be able to register the existence of the new idea. Doing so would require loosening his grip on beliefs so thoroughly interwoven with emotion that letting go of them would be viewed as "death": death of a closely held, tightly gripped – but limited – identity. This happens to all of us, much more than we like to admit.

Ideology is characterized largely by generalization: it provides narrow explanations for experiences an individual has, and then declares those explanations to be relevant to similar experiences happening to different people or over time to the same person. That's similar to what theories do, but with the critical difference mentioned above: ideologies protect themselves, at all costs, from being tested. They fend off any notion of independently checking the truth of their constructs. Those in power who shelter ideology from examination do so to entrench their position. Their proclaimed interest is truth, but their actual interest is power. They get away with it because ideologies that make some sense of experience provide a welcome relief to a person overwhelmed by having to think his way through every situation he faces. Being overwhelmed in this way is more a reflection of psychological factors than it is of intelligence factors. Plenty of smart people subscribe to ideologies; what has gone missing in such people is the solidity of identity necessary to remain open to life's mysteries, and to entertain doubt without becoming psychologically paralyzed.

Somewhere along this continuum, determined largely by the intensity of psychological need an individual has, he may take a further step: into fundamentalism. This is the *third tipping point* on the continuum. The psychological factors that sway him to do so include things such as the influence he attributes to the ideology for any improvements to his life. Does he perceive that his psychological needs are being met? Does he experience empowerment? How indebted does he feels towards his new surrogate family?

Fundamentalism is the point on the continuum where ideologies really get hyper-organized. It is the point where a person willingly seeks to convert others because he has absolute certainty about the truth of his ideology. If the metaphor for ideology is calcification, the metaphor for fundamentalism is totalitarianism: rigidity taken to its extreme, disallowing of dissent, putting rules in place to explain every aspect of existence, and imposing an absolute authority to oversee the implementation of these rules. Because it is further along the persuasion continuum than ideology, fundamentalism can provide even greater relief than the certainty someone initially embracing ideology experiences. This certainty feels total. The temptation to turn off critical thinking is even greater.

The narrowing that occurs when a person becomes fundamentalist can occur in any conceptual arena. Religion, politics, and economics are three areas typically associated with fundamentalism. Ideological tentacles, however, reach everywhere ideas have been organized to provide a comprehensive view of things: health, education, the environment, art, parenting, human rights, psychology, and science, for instance. No system of thought is immune from human beings imposing on top of it something more extreme: something that reflects a person's needs for power, identity, or belonging. Fundamentalism is the extreme organizational extension of ideology.

Re-examining the persuasion continuum was helpful for me because it re-attuned me to the gradualness of how swoons capture people. That gradualness highlighted why mindful presence and respectful, challenging but supportive relationships with others are needed to track any slides down the continuum.

27 Krsnamurti, *First and Last Freedom*, p. 46
28 Saul, p.142
29 Sartres, p.63
30 Festinger, p. 203 - 210.
31 Pradine in Strongman, p. 20
32 Sartre in Sontag, p. 97

Chapter 7

Meditation Without Dogma

Be patient toward all that is unsolved in your heart and try to love the questions themselves, like locked rooms and like books that are written in a foreign tongue.

Do not now seek the answers, which cannot yet be given you because you would not yet be able to live them.

And the point is, to live everything.
Live the questions now.
Perhaps you will then gradually, without noticing it, live along some distant day into the answer.

- Rainer Marie Rilke

As I turned my attention to how I could pursue self-knowledge without an ideological framework, I was acutely aware of how difficult this would be. The only thing I knew for sure was that I wanted all three levels of identity to be part of whatever process I undertook: the personal, my immediate family/friends/colleagues, and the wider community. The difficulty of this work stemmed in part from my underestimation of the simple, straightforward nature of what was necessary: anything that would allow me to sustain my awareness in the present moment.

Staying in the present is not complicated, but it's extraordinarily difficult. There was no need to search far and wide for new techniques to use to accomplish this; what I had to do was simply persevere with things I already knew how to do. I focused my attention on two processes: one I had learned from my meditation practice, and the other from the psychological work I had done.

Over the years, these two processes slowly but surely nudged me in the direction of increasing my self-knowledge. The first process was to strengthen my capacity to take a step back from personal identity and witness my behavior. I had observed this technique of *mindful witnessing* in Buddhist, Hindu, Quaker and Taoist approaches to self-knowledge. The second process was to renew my commitment to relate directly and honestly to other people: to do so without sabotaging myself through expectations, beliefs, or strategies. In other words, to engage in *authentic relationships*. Understanding the importance of authentic relationships had resulted from years of individual psychotherapy, group psychotherapy, and my provision of both to others.

The demands of both these practices reflect a reality every person faces in an increasingly globalized world: the recognition that the consequence of every action he takes is increasing in significance, not the other way around. What an individual does matters. As the globalized world brings people into more contact with each other, as organizations become increasingly dysfunctional, individual actions become more important. If those actions are exercised in mindful ways, characterized by authentic relationships, the capacity for people to move away from ideological processes and towards self-knowledge will increase the likelihood of transformative social change. Proponents of ideologies scoff at the simplicity of this, largely because their power grows when they are able to convince people that their secret handshake models are the only solution to humanity's problems.

Their success in demeaning mindful witnessing and authentic relationships, combined with the difficulty of doing both skillfully, has made it much easier to put these very practical tools to the side. They're also ignored by some because they seem too uncomplicated.

This belies that fact that both these methods awaken awareness in ways that take time and commitment, and which require the capacity to learn from mistakes made along the way. These two approaches emerged from the rubble of my ideological pursuits and challenged me to make use of what they had to offer. I knew they had consistently helped me trust my inner compass and assert sovereignty over my life so far, so there was no reason to doubt that would change in the future. Since mindful witnessing is the one I learned about first I'll describe how it worked for me, knowing as I do so that volumes of more detailed information about it exists in the spiritual traditions cited above.

The ability to witness one's life from a distance is an incredibly powerful impetus to transformation. Doing so successfully offers a person the same balcony perspective as a caregiver mirroring his child through that child's narcissistic explorations. The difference as an adult is that this mirroring state of consciousness is accessed by the person himself, instead of having it provided by someone outside himself.

The witness is an aspect of consciousness available to everyone. Available, but not personal. It's not personal because it's not part of personal identity. This is sometimes difficult for people to accept because accessing the witness begins through exercising personal will. In doing so, it may seem as though the witness is part of identity. To assume this would be a mistake, however, because it is the capacity to be detached from identity and to neutrally observe all the activities engaged in by identity that define the witness. The irony of such detachment is that the willingness to employ it depends on the person having enough confidence in the solidity of his identity to be willing to create distance from it and witness it. This is one of the most potent experiments a human being can undertake.

The witness is a bridge that brings a person into the present, into direct experience, and into greater contact with who and what is around him. Whatever comes into the field of awareness is fair game for the witness: external events, internal events, states of consciousness, assumed roles, even how awareness itself operates. The witness observes all of this in a heightened yet unemotional way, well beyond the limited perspective possible through personal identity. When a person decides to access the witness, he accesses much broader levels of awareness. If he learns to sustain that awareness, he experiences the world around and inside him in a more panoramic, in-depth way.

The witness is analogous to breathing: it is always present and is always operating, but is so "ordinary" it is taken for granted. Breathing happens in the body but is not part of the body. Through exercising personal will awareness can be moved to the witness, just as breathing patterns can be altered through exercising will. Because of this, and because becoming skilled in establishing consciousness in the witness helps to protect a person from any emotional hijacks he may be susceptible to, witnessing is an altered state of consciousness that is not driven by belief nor susceptible to emotion. This is what makes the witness the ideal platform for the transformation of identity. The witness does not care one way or another about the events observed; it does not care how they are observed; it does not care how actions a person does or doesn't take turn out; and it doesn't care if transformation occurs. Its only function is to notice things. This neutrality and singularity of function make the witness an ideal portal to greater self-knowledge.

When the witness is not accessed, a person engages his consciousness from the platform of whatever identity he has either adopted or discovered. In the case of an adopted identity, this platform is unsteady. A person living through an adopted identity knows that at some level he is pretending, and is continually anxious about being caught out. This usually impels him to push his awareness outward for another identity that feels more real. Since the whole process is externally oriented, his identity decisions are more likely to be guided by emotional impulse than by a quieter sense of inner knowing. Embracing such stimulation allows a person to escape the work of discovering who he might be. It allows identity to skip emotionally, and superficially, from one imaginary version of self to another.

When a person operates from discovered identity, on the other hand, the witness has usually played a role in making this possible. Once a person has the experience of discovering identity, he learns to trust his reflective capacity. He is much more likely, as a result, to take a step back from whatever his identity is and move to the witness. Perhaps the memory of being witnessed by another is in operation, or perhaps it is a lack of desperate clinging to whatever his identity at the moment might be. Whatever the reason, once the witness is accessed it brings a bigger awareness forward - an awareness that has a dissipative power.

How does this dissipative power work? When the witness notices, for example, some form of contracted awareness in a person – perhaps a painful repressed memory – the non-emotional spotlight it shines on that contraction is fearless. When that fearless spotlight of neutral awareness is focused on a contracted part of a person's psyche, it loosens the hold that contraction – and all the memories, emotions and beliefs it may contain – has on him. This is a foundational principle of meditation. Meditation practitioners know that unadorned awareness has this power, which is why most forms of meditation involve cultivation of the witness in some way. By applying the witness repeatedly over time, this dissipative power is accessed more frequently. A person increases the likelihood that he will become less identified with false notions of who he is. When a person learns to trust witnessing, when he learns to be comfortable in this altered state of consciousness, the dissipative power of awareness that is unlocked will, on occasion, lead to identity deconstruction. This is often followed by the reconstruction of a larger, more aware self-concept. The witness triggers this process.

Each of the identities a person discovers this way is impermanent, although each surrounds and connects him to a core sense of I-ness. Eastern philosophies argue that this core sense of I-ness is also illusory, and that the ultimate spiritual goal for a person is to disidentify from this as well if he wishes to become enlightened. An ambition to achieve permanent enlightenment, however, requires adopting ideological concepts that deflect a person away from the necessary construction of a solid identity in the present. As mentioned earlier, some spiritual ideologies demonize identity construction as a harmful illusion. This ignores the fact that any attempt to short circuit the construction of identity avoids the work of functioning capably in the wider world. Assuming that a person doesn't sidestep this work, he will embark on a process of discovering new, more comprehensive forms of identity over time: a process that doesn't end. He does this through enlarging awareness; he integrates what he's discovered with his core sense of self. This enables him to deal with increasingly complex circumstances, and to become a fuller human being in the process.

Life will continue to present any person with situations his current identity not only hasn't faced before, but which require something new from him. There's no guarantee these will lead to transformation, of course, and life is full of people applying the same strategies they've always used to new problems and then wondering why their timeworn approach just doesn't work. Opportunities for transformation presented through life circumstances throw a person the challenge of witnessing identity and allowing it to deconstruct. Deconstruction of identity is synonymous with a willingness to enter an ideology-free zone of exploration, not just through reflection, but through the second means I have used in my own quest for self-knowledge: relating directly and honestly to others without expectation, strategic intent, or belief getting in the way.

Forming authentic relationships requires much braver interpersonal skills than those employed in ideological environments. That bravery is a product of a solid identity well connected to a person's inner compass. It helps considerably if a person has learned to trust others in the process of allowing identity to emerge. If he is accustomed to adopting identity externally, he relates to others primarily in a strategic way. He spends a disproportionate amount of time pushing away genuine contact to shield his own perceived vulnerabilities, and to meet his own psychological needs. This approach requires cleverness not courage; it bases itself on relationships forged in the mind rather than in the world. Strategically forged relationships are what have spawned the volumes of literature on how people objectify each other; i.e. how they relate in ways that avoid contact and focus on self-interest. Relating in this manner is a superficial, performance - oriented way of dealing with others. Relationships become impression management. Whenever relationships are based on ideas about people rather than on a direct experience of them, the abstraction that results takes a person further from, not closer to, his inner compass.

Authentic relationships are based, at a minimum, on non-defended vulnerability, curiosity about others and the courage to disagree. All three of these qualities are essential to connect with another person. As with mindful witnessing, this approach doesn't sound complicated enough to experts hawking their ideology. Concluding this ignores the fact that forging authentic relationships through cultivating these qualities requires time, commitment, and daily practice. Simple does not mean easy, especially given the reality that building such relationships inevitably involves failures along the way. The failure to find the courage to contradict another person. The failure to display vulnerability. The failure to be willing to operate outside one's own self-interests in a relationship.

Of the minimum qualities necessary for authentic relationship, curiosity is the least threatening to most people. Even this quality is in short supply when a person is functioning ideologically, however. Curiosity in an ideological context is confined to matters that support the advance of the ideology. This is considerably different from the curiosity necessary for enhanced self-knowledge, which involves a willingness to explore unknown territory simply to learn something new. I only understood the importance of vulnerability, curiosity, and a willingness to disagree when I looked back at my Ananda Marga years and considered how people within the organization, including myself, related to each other at the time.

Those relationships were built on a fervent desire to foster like-mindedness. The primary consequence of that desire was to undermine authenticity at every turn. Every interaction was filtered through an ideological lens that created either superficial acquiescence, saccharine intimacy or righteous indignation: all devoid of bravery. Relationships steered well clear of overt conflict, succumbing to a push for conformity that drove genuine disagreement underground. Instead of encouraging a person to relate to others based on an inner sense of determining what's appropriate to a situation – and to be willing not just to fight but to learn from whoever he is communicating with - he is expected to use relationships as another opportunity to reinforce ideological perspectives.

This happened regularly in Ananda Marga. On one dramatic occasion, however, I observed a powerful exception. This was during the second Maha, when the PROUT organizers confronted all the participants with a challenge. They informed us that the Indian government had finally gone too far in oppressing Ananda Marga. Jailing the guru had been one thing, but closing down all the organization's social service projects in India was clearly another. The Indian government was trying to push Ananda Marga over the edge, and it was the responsibility of the organization in the U.S. to do something about it.

The "something" they suggested was to break into the Indian Embassy in Seattle after hours. Our task would then be to ransack their files, pour chicken blood on the ones related to Ananda Marga in protest, and notify the press of our actions for publicity purposes. The PROUT leaders then began to indicate who would perform what role in carrying out this mission.

It was at that point that one of our group members stood his ground against this plan. "I'm not pouring chicken blood on anything. And I'm not going to be part of any illegal embassy break-in." The whole room immediately went silent. This man had articulated a response to the discomfort shared in the minds of many of us who were too timid to do so ourselves. He had found the courage to confront the authorities running the Maha and to hold his ethical ground. It was a brave thing to do in a context that until that point had been completely controlled by the organizers.

Once their authority was challenged, however, the organizers exulted. "Good work!" they exclaimed. "We've been waiting for someone to stand up to us all week! This demonstrates your growing strength...," etc. We were led to believe that we had been put through the paces of this mini-psychodrama to challenge us on our own courage. What had actually happened was that our brave member's stand had caught the organizers on the wrong foot, forcing them to back off their original plans and pretend that this had been their intention all along. The courage of one person to stand up to the organizers was a powerful lesson to all of us: be fearless in the face of conflict when your integrity is at stake. Operate from a solid sense of identity, connected to your inner compass. This man's courage also confirmed that no matter how much ideological pressure is placed on a person, he is still capable of acting from his own sovereignty at any point.

Finding the courage to seize interpersonal opportunities and developing the skills to relate straightforwardly without defensiveness moves a person powerfully in the direction of self-knowledge. It reduces a person's susceptibility to conversion by pre-empting the creation of trance states. There's nothing so useful as constructive, respectful conflict for throwing an elephant in a person's puddle: a task every person needs done to him from time to time. Doing this work clarifies the difference between a relationship that is real and one that is based on expectations, beliefs and strategies. If vulnerability, curiosity, and courage can be fostered in relationship, there is no need for either party to convert the other to his beliefs to feel secure.

Another way of saying this is that authentic relationships are only developed in organizational environments that support people to test identity in relationship. This requires risk taking and vulnerability not just by members but also by the authorities in the organization. It requires more rigor in monitoring how relationships are going, and acting on that awareness. This is next to impossible when an organization's ideology hinges on its members adhering to clearly outlined hierarchical relationships. Even more so if the ultimate relationship advocated is an abstract one with a personal god who is always above the person, and whose representative is an organizational authority. When the latter is the case, the courage needed to confront the injustices that inevitably appear in the organization is undermined by the abstract nature of the ultimate authority.

Promoting abstract spiritual relationships ahead of pragmatic real ones diverts relationship problems underground. When these problems surface later, there is no mechanism in place to deal with them. This gap has been glaring apparent in religious organizations over the years through the numerous examples of their authorities sexually abusing children in their care. Those within the organization who protected perpetrators or pretended the behavior didn't exist epitomize the cowardice ideological authorities display when they have to confront real relationship problems. Ignoring authentic relationships includes not preparing for the fallout that results when manipulative, power-over ways of interacting are the norm.

The avoidance of the work necessary to forge authentic relationships includes a disinterest in psychotherapeutic processes. Such processes skillfully employed are grounded in present time, and are a tremendously effective way to increase mindful awareness. They require that people respect and inhabit their worldly identities, however: including all the flaws that characterize those identities. This is the reason for their unpopularity. The mindfulness gained psychotherapeutically often runs through a gauntlet of considerable discomfort and conflict. Navigating such a path has no appeal to a person ideologically geared towards concepts such as enlightenment or perfection. This lack of interest allows the vast majority of people in both secular and spiritual organizations to take refuge in adopted identities; to put forward performances that impress. This may reflect hard work, but it lacks the depth characterizing both a discovered identity and authentic relationships. Both are essential foundation stones necessary for pursuing self-knowledge. Having a strong identity heightens a person's awareness of the value of addressing psychological matters, and increases his willingness to do so in relationship. It encourages a person to be braver about testing himself through interacting with others. Organizations have become incredibly sophisticated in the ways such tests are avoided. This is usually done through the creation of spaghetti bureaucracies which always defer responsibility for a person's actions to abstractions: the limits of his role, for instance, or the ease with which he can claim incomplete knowledge as a screen to hide behind.

One reason it is rare to see authentic relationships valued in most contemporary organizations is that the dominant meta-narratives pay them no heed whatsoever. This amplifies the difficulty of creating authentic relationships, because doing so requires challenging concepts at the core of the Frontier and Protestant Reformation meta-narratives: extreme individualism, perfection, limitlessness, and the self-inflation accompanying any notion of being chosen, saved or enlightened. The dominant meta-narratives have been influential in determining how people structure their lives for a long time; that influence includes how people view the way they relate to each other. Dealing authentically with conflict inside an organization based on either the Frontier or Protestant Reformation meta-narrative might mean, for example, the simple but threatening act of exposing the consequences of power differentials between those with positional authority and those without it: particularly if the latter have better insight into how to deal with the problems the organization faces. It might mean confronting the inflation of the organization's authorities publicly, which runs the unthinkable risk of undercutting the image the organization has manufactured. It might mean unearthing the self-loathing a person carries beneath the outward bliss he projects in his spiritual persona, which could lead to exposing deeper ethical problems in an organization. Because the alliance most organizations have made with the Protestant work ethic means they prioritize productivity ahead of authenticity, all of these types of problems – ones where impression making has the highest value – are apt to occur regularly. Operating outside of the mindset put forward by the dominant meta-narratives automatically places a person in a fringe category, and usually out of a job.

Even if a person is willing to take that particular risk, however, the psychological difficulty of breaking free of the influence of the meta-narratives in order to build authentic relationship and cultivate mindful witnessing is enormous. This is partly a matter of habit, partly a matter of the weight of so many people doing things as per convention, and partly a matter of how invisible the meta-narratives have become. This last feature is particularly important: the influence of the meta-narratives lies largely with their invisibility. Even when an ideology stemming from them is clearly visible, the underpinning meta-narrative isn't unless a harder look is taken. This invisibility accounts for the difficulty groups vehemently opposed to them *conceptually* have when it comes to actually contradicting their influence *behaviorally*.

How, for instance, could an organization intent on the most radical change possible – political revolution – end up exhibiting behavior exemplifying the same meta-narratives characterizing the society it is trying to change? This is what happened to the Weather Underground in the 60s. The Weather Underground prided itself on its commitment to overthrow the U.S. government and radically confront the American way of life. This candid quote from former member Mark Rudd, reflecting a time of crises within the organization, indicates the prevailing organizational attitude at the time:

> "At that point in our thinking, there were no innocent Americans, at least not among the white ones. They all played some part in the atrocities of Viet Nam, if only the passive roles of ignorance,

acquiescence, and acceptance of privilege. All guilty. All Americans were legitimate targets for attack. We wanted this country to taste a tiny bit of what it had been dishing out. Just like the passive Americans we derided, I acquiesced in this terrible, demented logic. Not only was I willing to take the risks and suffer the consequences, but more importantly, I was overwhelmed by hate. I cherished my hate, as a badge of moral superiority."[33]

The irony of this attitude is not lost on its author, who retrospectively recognizes that despite the organization's commitment to change, something had gone terribly wrong. The consumptive anger experienced by Rudd and others in revolutionary movements demonstrates how easily narcissistic rage and puritanical self-righteousness can influence a person's behavior, even when that person believes his values run contrary to the society's dominant meta-narratives. Rage and righteousness overwhelm access to the witness, undermine a person's capacity to form authentic relationships with those seen as enemies, and put a fractured identity back in control. The result is many things done which are later looked upon with regret. Relationships are filtered through emotionalized belief and "demented logic" wins the day: particularly if a person has taken the additional step of operating ideologically.

When the beliefs of an ideologue are pushed to the wall, the failure of his actions to produce the results expected of him can prompt narcissistic rage to erupt instantaneously. His adoption of the ideology will have included the identity that comes with it, all of which points to narcissistic damage hiding behind a thin wall of a public persona. The eruption that can occur is not confined to groups who are of any particular ideological bent. Mainstream institutions are just as susceptible as revolutionary organizations are. What leads to a person's susceptibility to narcissistic rage is his embrace of any ideology combined with a less than solidly grounded identity. The frightening conclusion that this points to is that a person with a high level of positional authority who is operating ideologically can unleash enormous destructive power – including the power a mainstream but narcissistic politician has in directing state violence towards perceived enemies. If his actions are fueled by emotionalized identities constructed to protect beliefs instead of by a neutral accounting of the facts; if he opposes an open-minded dialogue with the parties affected; or if his personal capacity to tolerate ambiguity and paradox is damaged, the result is actions taken that create more problems than originally existed. The manner in which the Weather Underground went to war with the United States in the 1960s and the manner in which the United States went to war in Iraq in 2003 may look different politically, but they both demonstrate how the overlay between ideological thinking and narcissistic damage distorts facts and leads to irrational behavior.

Another way ideological thinking undermines the witness and authentic relationships is when adherents to that ideology express a sense of moral superiority. Moral superiority is a reflection of ideological absolutism; it is an indication that a person has traveled far enough along the persuasion continuum to have become fundamentalist. Moral superiority is central to puritanism and its descendants, despite the language of humility publicly adopted over the years to suggest otherwise. It reflects a person's desire to be "pure" in his thinking, in the same way the puritans themselves desired to be. The distance from puritan insistence that a person cannot be flexible with the word of God to an attitude of moral superiority is a short one. Once an ideology is locked down firmly, the certainty it generates leads to arrogance in all areas of life, including absolutist notions of what's right and what isn't. The fact that elements of counter-societal movements such as the Weather Underground succumbed to this sort of moral superiority emphasized again to me how widespread, effective, and unconscious the influences of the dominant meta-narratives are, especially in combination with psychological vulnerability. The strength of the meta-narratives, and their hold on the human psyche, is much tighter than most people imagine.

The passive acceptance of a meta-narrative's ideas over time is not just a tribute to their invisibility. It also reflects how easily people can take false comfort in the notion of viewing fundamentalist behavior as something "out there," done by extremists. While the weave between meta-narratives, ideology, and ultimately fundamentalism can be loose or tight, circumstances, intent and even accidents can instantly change all that.

This phenomenon was explored by research into terrorism conducted by Marc Sageman. Sageman became interested after 9-11 in how terrorist cells are formed by middle eastern expatriates and their offspring in European countries. His "bunch of guys" theory[34] was an explanation of this phenomenon. The gist of this theory is that a certain proportion of expatriates in their new countries come together, bonded by their desire for friendship and community, meeting in places such as mosques and, at times, forming terrorist cells from the kinship that develops and the common grievances shared against perceived oppressors. Interestingly, Sageman's research points out that the people joining together in this way aren't directly recruited by a religious organization. Rather, they spontaneously organize. Once they do, group dynamics emphasizing common grievances can take hold. Depending on the psychological need, the fractured sense of identity, and the desperation the group feels, it can be a short step from there to the consideration of violence as a means of expressing such grievances. Importantly, Sageman concludes that the terrorists he studied *were as psychologically healthy as people in the mainstream population.*

Dr. Ariel Merari[35] the founder and former commander of the Israeli Defense Force's Hostage Negotiation and Crises Management Team, later a researcher at Tel Aviv University's Study of Political Violence, also concluded that the majority of people who become terrorists have psychological health equivalent to that of the mainstream population.

What does the psychological health of those who join extremist groups – combined with the evidence that such groups are now forming of their own accord – indicate about how ideology works? The normalcy of people who join organizations deemed fringe or terrorist is not a shock to anyone who has been in such an organization. Media generated "loner" theories have never made sense. They are based on shallow, mainstream definitions of normalcy that have been adopted unthinkingly. How many stories of "normal" people doing horrible things are needed to rectify this? Many people considered normal are able, to all outward appearances, function capably in work and society – but may domestically abuse their spouse behind closed doors, secretly engage in deeply rooted addictive behaviors, or go out on a murder spree lasting months or years. Normalcy descriptions say nothing of the inside world of the person. They say nothing about the person's perception of the society he lives in, his levels of frustration, the quality of his relationships, or the meaningfulness of his life.

What they do indicate is how disinterested, or perhaps fearful, people really are in making the effort to understand one another at anything other than a superficial level. Societal blindness to what lies behind outward appearances of normalcy are an indictment pointing to how vacuous most relationships people have with each other are, and how self-absorbed society has become. That blindness fails to recognize that the collective loss of interest in anything beyond surface appearances signifies that society has lost its bearings, and is ignoring the clues and the work necessary to right itself.

Sageman's observation that groups are spontaneously organizing into terrorist cells raises important questions. The trend to spontaneously organize would seem to reflect a depth of rage people who view themselves as outside the mainstream feel towards society, a belief that things are terribly wrong. What is its source? Is it isolation? Has that isolation reached such extremes that joining a fundamentalist organization doesn't even require a sales pitch any more? Is it identity? Has securing a real identity become so difficult that conversion to anything is seen as a better option than living in the confused, directionless state of "going through the motions" on a daily basis? Is it the wealth divide? Has poverty penetrated the lives of so many people that revolting against the system is considered a "nothing to lose" proposition? Is it the spiritual vacuity of modern day life? Does that emptiness indicate how spiritually meaningless the ambitious pursuit of wealth has become?

There is truth to all of these views, and undoubtedly to others. Regardless of whether these reasons or others are responsible, however, the spontaneous organization of oppositional groups without a focused conversion attempt – especially given the successful track record of conversion-based organizations – signals how frustrated people are, usually unconsciously, with how their lives have been shaped by the meta-narratives and the ideologies they spawn. Any number of political and social groups, past and present, left and right, continues to reflect the widespread nature of this discontent.

The outward manifestations of the meta-narratives are what people react against, but the depth of work necessary to unwrap their influence on the psychological, social, and spiritual worlds of those doing the protesting is seldom appreciated. All three levels of identity have to be addressed if a person is to make genuine progress to extricate himself from the influence of the dominant meta-narratives. Whatever methods a person uses to do this, he will need to cultivate an ability to sustain presence of mind and a willingness to engage in authentic relationships.

Using these tools instigates a process of *unlearning* rather than one of taking on something new. It appreciates the fact that the damage inflicted by ideological movements rooted in the dominant meta-narratives has been built up over a long period of time. The dominance of the Frontier and Protestant Reformation meta-narratives are what gave unrestrained self-interest its compelling momentum. The groundwork these meta-narratives laid gave fundamentalism, religious and secular, traction and influence. Both of them fostered the polarities characterizing the contemporary world – between rich and poor, between the sinner and the saved, between the powerful and the powerless. Buying into the ideologies that sprang from these meta-narratives has meant individuals and societies everywhere have succumbed to small, then large, degrees of incremental self-deception. This has resulted in people allowing fear and insecurity to erode an ethical sense, to undermine commitment to the common good, to allow their identity to be predominantly shaped by external forces, and to replace the pursuit of self-knowledge with the pursuit of personal ambition.

Nowhere is this more evident than in the truce the Protestant work ethic brokered between frontier driven prosperity and puritan notions of the innate sinfulness of all people. This combination has driven personal ambition so deeply into the central nervous system of U.S. society that credible opposition to the unbridled pursuit of wealth has, until recently, been in intensive care. Until the 2007 recession, for example, news such as unwarranted executive bonuses or the massive wealth accrued by a small segment of society hardly registered a blip on the radar of most people. It played a distant second fiddle to the desire among the majority of the society's members to replicate that wealth for themselves: and the belief that they could. That aspiration has pushed forward an acceptance of the notions of progress and growth as always positive.

The damage wreaked by both meta-narratives now appears to be a house of cards collapsing under the weight of its own excess. Structuring society around the Frontier meta-narrative's hyper-individualism and puritanism's self-righteous certainty, then balancing these on narcissistic injury that scours any environment it comes in contact with for the latest identity to adopt produces a superficiality, a falseness, that people are increasingly unwilling to accept. Encouraging though this trend may be, picking through the rubble generated during the heyday of these meta-narratives continues to turn up evidence of how poisonous the full-hearted embrace of them has been.

That poison is particularly damaging when it produces ideologies that are utopian in nature, as mentioned earlier. The finality promised by utopian aspirations has fueled a huge portion of the destruction that has taken place in the world over its history, a mistake repeated over many centuries but now with considerably less room to absorb its consequences. Elegant theoretical propositions, the mimicry of authenticity, a focus on perfection, self-righteous certainty and the promise of a conflict-free future are a lethal combination of factors that most people find alluring at some point in life, usually more than once. Allowing oneself the indulgence of hanging up one's thinking cap and swaying in the most attractive emotional breeze, however, is a luxury that the finiteness and interconnectedness of the world now prohibits.

What would the world look if the dominant meta-narratives no longer held sway? What would it be like if people increased flexibility and tolerance of ambiguity to the point where it wasn't necessary to turn off thinking and turn to ideology? How would the pursuit of self-knowledge play out if action in the world were characterized more by Pradine's notion of sentiment rather than by emotional excitation? Or if interconnectedness instead of competition was the primary lens through which people were viewed? What would happen if people made efforts to value self-knowledge for its own sake - including its collective pursuit? If people were inspired by ideals but refused to become ideologues?

If the freedom people initially felt in the early stages of the Protestant Reformation and Frontier meta-narratives has run its course, these questions will have the space necessary to be explored in the wider society. In doing so, it is critical not to dismiss the numerous benefits that the dominant meta-narratives have provided society, irrespective of their shortfalls. Benefits such as the recognition that a person has the power to shape his own destiny, or that it is worth his time to make the effort to have a personal relationship with something larger than his personality, or the value of cultivating a willingness to take on seemingly impossible challenges: these are not to be minimized. They have served to move society forward in countless ways. The problem lies in the absolutism grafted onto the central ideas of these meta-narratives, and the sovereignty a person sacrifices when he chooses that absolutism over authenticity. It is not a case of the dominant meta-narratives not having value for people; it's a case of that value being elevated beyond its usefulness.

Seeing the problems currently facing society clearly requires regaining the perspective necessary to explore bigger questions in a constructive way. That means breaking the cycle of replacing one ideology with another as the way of doing so. It means being alert to how the persuasion continuum works, and interrupting a gradual descent into ideology by witnessing one's life with greater mindfulness. It means not letting the starting points of inspiration be co-opted by ideologies eager to narrow the underlying meta-narratives. Underestimating all of these things causes people to overlook the ever-present threat of fundamentalism, a threat characterized by two chilling realities. 1) The fact that fundamentalists will do *anything*, law-abiding or lawbreaking, life-giving or life-destroying, to impose their ideology on others, and 2) A failure to recognize how much the collective passivity of vast numbers of people has already allowed ideological approaches to life to penetrate and establish themselves not only institutionally, but psychologically.

Wherever passivity, living dogmatically and unhealed psychological damage coexist, they create a susceptibility to the endless drip-fed of the conversion process, to ideology, and to fundamentalism. At the moment, very few people are aware how connected their behavior is to a tacit acceptance of outdated meta-narratives embedded in psychological damage, propped up by strategic rather than authentic relationships. This has resulted in an almost universal failure to see how many areas of life are steered by one sort of ideology or another.

Examples of ideology morphing into fundamentalist extremism will increase the more the current meta-narratives collapse. This collapse represents a desperate grab for certainty in the face of an increasing number of people who no longer wish to function ideologically. It clings to the limited notion of fighting fire with fire, and does its best to persuade people to deceive themselves the way I did into thinking they are doing something oppositional rather than repeating the same pattern under a different guise. Radical Islamists are the headline example of this, pitting their fundamentalism against injustices the populations they live in have legitimately experienced in a showdown whose drama plays out daily on our television screens. As long as enough people ignore this trend towards ideological extremism, sanction governments to respond solely with violence, bury their heads in the individual accumulation of wealth, or passively turn away from the dilemmas society itself has created and labels them "too hard," the choices available will be limited to one fundamentalism or the other. That is no choice at all.

The alternative is to take a non-ideological road back from the limping meta-narratives. That is unlikely to be anything other than a gut-wrenching but occasionally inspirational process, and probably much more gradual than most people would prefer. Unfortunately, tolerance for gradual processes has diminished as acceptance of the dictates of the Protestant Reformation and Frontier meta-narratives – and the fruits produced by economic rationalism – has deepened. Combined with technological advances that have accelerated the pace at which everyone lives in the world people now want change instantly, without the hard work such change requires. People have become consumers of change because initiating it in one's self, through genuine interactions with others, has become such an unfamiliar process. This leads to change that is shallow rather than deep, frequent rather than brave, and hooked on the various transcendent rushes garnered from superficial success in areas such as wealth accumulation or the infamous pursuit of "15 minutes of fame." These are pursued without any thought to the compromises in integrity that more often than not accompany such prosperity or acclaim.

The lasting change required to operate outside the meta-narratives is more difficult now than it was 35 years ago for a number of reasons: one is that there has been a huge increase in resources devoted to the conversion process. Mainstream resources such as advertising agencies, marketing firms, government advisors, media consultancies, public relations firms, spin doctors, and so on work furiously to bend people to their ways. Layer upon layer of people hired with one aim: to convert people to a product, an ideology, a cause, or a movement.

It's also more difficult because operating outside the meta-narratives and the conversion process means reversing society's increasing inability to conduct trustworthy, in-depth dialogue in public arenas, with honest differences of opinion freely expressed, without any ulterior motive or collapses into a self-righteous refusal to consider alternatives. Most adults in the world today would be cynical about society's capacity for doing this in a sustained way. It points to the glaring deficit society has in engaging in authentic relationships. Instead, we have become accustomed to being surrounded by a planet full of salespeople selling a product, a religion, an organization, a leader, a government policy, etc. In every field of endeavor this sales pitch has intensified, replacing societal norms more protective of collective well being. This campaign has been aggressively instituted in societies around the globe and people have, for the most part, either steered themselves out of the way or aligned themselves with ideologies destined to repeat the same problems should they get the chance to do so.

The story I've been telling in these chapters outlines my own struggles with these issues back in an era where the urgency for change was intense, but no more so than in the very wired and much more global present. Its details include some of the many times in which I ignored my own awareness in deference to the ideas of someone else. This process today may be accelerated, it may look different on the outside, it may be more extreme - but underlying all this it bears a striking resemblance in process and principle to the experiences I've recalled in these pages. Increasingly, and optimistically, more people are dissatisfied with a world focused one-dimensionally on individual success and material well being above all other concerns. Changing that focus will require attending to the pursuit of genuine self-knowledge in a substantive way. The cultivation of self-knowledge is the single most powerful means of moving both self and society in a different direction.

I still work in my own way to change things I don't like in the world, but my Ananda Marga years taught me a crucial lesson about doing so: to be aware of how quickly a good idea can intensify and change instantly into some form of calcified extremism. Extremism fueled by emotionalized belief putting forward overly simplistic solutions to complicated issues. I am aware of the need to continually make efforts to strengthen my immunity to conversion and to its byproduct: fundamentalism of all kinds – in particular, the narrowing of god or any notion of spirituality.

This does not mean abandoning the notion of believing strongly in an idea, or to stop advocating for ideas. It certainly doesn't mean not believing in anything. Acting from belief, based on accumulated experience and the conclusions drawn from those experiences, will always be the way most people function most of the time. What's being suggested here is the importance of increasing presence. This in turn leads to the openness and flexibility necessary to gain distance from beliefs with regularity. Calling belief-based actions into question to better tolerate ambiguity, navigate through complexity, transform identity if need be, and relate to people fearlessly instead of ideologically. All of these are ways to move life more towards the quiet horizon of the present moment. In a world changing as rapidly as ours is, a world requiring new ways of considering things because the problems we face are increasingly complex, not doing this is an oversight with enormous consequences.

Neither of the two tools I've mentioned for resisting conversion provide a foolproof firewall against falling back into actions based on the meta-narratives, narcissistic injury, surrogate communities, or intensity-laced rituals that emotionally excite and may, occasionally, provide fleeting moments of transcendence. I recognized this when I departed Ananda Marga, and it has since been confirmed many times. The confusion I was left with immediately after my departure was disabling in the extreme. To be honest, in the beginning I don't think I could have handled a job more complicated than pressure-cooking styrofoam containers for artificial breast implants. Occasionally, that confusion led to depressive episodes that lasted far longer than I would have wished. I suspect this type of scenario is the case for many who choose not to embrace ideologies. It can make for a difficult psychological existence because it plunges a person into existential loneliness and an increased susceptibility to the sense of worthlessness puritan ideology preys on wherever such loneliness exists. The vulnerability of such a state, however, also offers the possibility of a first step forward into greater awareness. Such a step is not possible when a person is comfortably certain of how the world works.

That certainty belies the reality of the current day world. As you, the reader, examine that world, ask yourself: Does it look like things are going well out there? Are people generally becoming kinder? More intelligent? Is community coming into balance with individual self-interest in a way that gives you hope for the future of your children? How does the physical environment look to you? What percentage of the news you read/listen to/ watch is focused on matters other than military and/or police activity of some sort? Despite our resources and knowledge, are people getting the health care they need when they are ill? Are you seeing increasing examples of people getting justice when their human rights have been taken away or infringed upon in some way? Are they getting the support of governments?

This list of questions could be longer, as you know. The answers to the issues they raise require a person to respond with courage and awareness – especially dogma-free spiritual awareness. Awareness willing to raise that most basic of questions, "Who am I?" and then actively respond to the echo this questions creates. There are more manuals on how to do this in the world than I could possibly list, wisdom of incredible value that doesn't need to be repeated here. I've limited myself to the two beginning steps that assisted me to begin to break the swoon of conversion I was in during the 70s.

I invite everyone reading this book to take the steps he knows are necessary to extricate himself from his own conversion swoons. Every ideology a person encounters – secular or religious, right or left – will entice him to do otherwise by giving him blueprint answers for the questions of life. No matter how much an idea rings true, however, it is only an idea. If it's acted on in lieu of recognizing the common humanity all of us share with people who have other ideas, if it's acted on from a dualistic framework of "us" and "them," then a person is responding not from a broader awareness but from psychological damage he has experienced to identity, or from meta-narratives he has adopted in lieu of independent thinking. More often than not, such actions carry with them a false moral certainty, susceptible at any moment to narcissistic rage, and captured by some notion of "pureness." They direct a person into ideological ghettos of false certainty, conformist superficiality, and deep-seated fear and loathing: of "outsiders," and ultimately of each other. Can global society afford this approach any longer?

Global society needs to move from the pat answers of ideologies to something more alive and creative. The need to do this pushes against efforts to convert people that increase daily in volume and sophistication and which, at their core, offer the false comforts of a non-thinking life. The alternative is simple but not specific, buoyed by the recognition that ideologies of any variety will always fall into the same trap: the trap of not trusting that human beings, if supported to develop a sense of ever-expanding identity, if encouraged to form authentic relationships with each other, if trusted to act from their own awareness instead of from an ideological map, will eventually find their way – and each other – in the process.

33   Rudd, unpublished memoirs
34   Sageman, throughout Understanding Terror Networks
35   Merari, throughout Terrorism and Threats to U.S. Interests in the Middle East.

Selected Bibliography

Anderson, Walter, *Reality Isn't What It Used to Be*, New York, Harper Collins, 1990.

Anonymous, *New England's First Fruit*, London, 1643 (1865 facsimile), as quoted in Wikipedia, Harvard University.

Angell, Engel and Hewitt, (pubs), *The Home Missionary*, in the Andover-Harvard Theological Library, Cambridge, 1850.

Banyard, Philip and Andrew Grayson, *Introducing Psychological Research*, New York, New York University Press, 1996.

Blass, Thomas, *The Man Who Shocked The World: The Life and Legacy of Stanley Milgram*, New York, Basic Books, 2004.

Bowttell, *Fighting A Political Virus*, in Griffith Review, 7, Autumn, 2005.

Bunyan, John, *The Pilgrim's Progress* (1678), New York, Oxford University Press, 1984.

Carroll, John, *Nihilistic Consequences of Humanism*, in "Griffith Review," 7, Autumn, 2005.

Carse, James P., *The Religious Case Against Belief*, New York, Penguin Books, 2008.

Collins, Randall, *Max Weber: A Skeleton Key*, London, Sage Publications, 1986.

Cook, C.M and Michael Persinger, *Experimental induction of the 'sensed presence' in normal subjects and an exceptional subject* in "Perceptual and Motor Skills," Vol 85, p 683, 1997.

Eliade, Mircea, *The Two and the One*, University of Chicago Press, 1979.

Ellenberger, Henri, *The Discovery of the Unconscious*, New York, Basic Books, 1970.

Festinger, L. and J. Carlsmith, *Cognitive Consequences of forced Compliance* in "Journal of Abnormal and Social Psychology," 58, 203 - 210, 1959.

Forrester, Duncan, *Apocalypse Now? Reflections on Faith in a Time of Terror*, Burlington, Ashgate Publishing, 2005.

Frank, Jerome, *Persuasion and Healing: A Comparative Study of Psychotherapy*, in "Persuasion, Coercion, Indoctrination and Mind Control," Zimbardo, Philip and Robert Vallone, Lexington, Ginn Custom, 1983.

Freud, Sigmund, *Civilisation and its Discontents*, New York, Norton, 2005 (reprint).

Giddens, Anthony, *Capitalism and Modern Social Theory*, London, Cambridge University Press, 1971.

Gray, John, *Black Mass: Apocalyptic Religion and the Death of Utopia*, New York, Farrar, Straus, and Giroux, 2007.

Harris, Sam, *Letter to a Christian Nation*, London, Bantam Press, 2007.

Hedges, Chris, *American Fascists*, New York, Free Press, 2006.

Hill, Christopher, *The World Turned Upside Down: Radical Ideas During the English Revolution*, New York, Penguin, 1975.

Hoffer, Eric, *The True Believer: Thoughts on the Nature of Mass Movements*, New York, Harper Brothers, 1951.

Hougan, Jim, *Decadence: Radical Nostalgia, Narcissism, and Decline in the Seventies*, New York, William Morrow, 1975.

Hotchkiss, Sandy, *Why is it Always About You?* New York, Free Press, 2002.

Huxley, Aldous, *The Perennial Philosophy*, New York, Harper Collins, 1945.

Jenkins, Philip, *Mystics and Messiahs*, New York, Oxford U. Press, 2000.

Johnson, Robert, *Balancing Heaven and Earth*, New York, Harper Collins, 1998.

Korzybski, Alfred, *A Non-Aristotelian System and its Necessity for Rigour in Mathematics and Physics* in "Science and Society," 1933.

Kramer, Joel and Alstad, Diana, *The Guru Papers: Masks of Authoritarian Power*, Berkeley, Frog Ltd, 1993.

Krsnamurti, J., *On Fear*, San Francisco, Harper, 1995.

Krsnamurti, J., *The First and Last Freedom*, New York, Harper Collins, 1975.

Lasch, Christopher, *The Culture of Narcissism: American Life in an Age of Diminishing Expectations*, New York, Norton, 1979.

Lasch, Christopher, *The Narcissist Society* in "The New York Review of Books," Vol. 23, Number 15, September 30, 1976.

Lifton, Robert J., *Thought Reform and the Psychology of Totalism*, North Carolina, U. of North Carolina Press, 1989.

Lasky, H.J., *The Dangers of Obedience*, in "Harper's Magazine," June, 1929.

Lofland, John and Rodney Stark, *Becoming A World Saver: A Theory of Conversion to a Deviant Perspective*, in "American Sociological Review," 30:862-875, 1965.

Lofland, John, *Becoming A World Saver Revisited*, in "American Behavioral Scientist," 20: 805-818, 1977.

McKay, Hugh, *Watching the Sparrow*, in "Griffith Review," 7, Autumn, 2005.

Merari, Dr. Ariel, *Terrorism and Threats to US Interests in the Mideast*, in "Hearing before the Special Oversight Panel on Terrorism of the Committee on Armed Services," U.S. House of Representatives, July 13, 2000.

Neitzsche, Friedrich, *The Gay Science* (translated by Walter Kaufmann), New York, Vintage, 1974

Newberg, Andrew and Eugene d'Aquili and Vince Rause, *Why God Won't Go Away*, New York, Ballantine, 2001

O'Sullivan, John, *The Great Nation of Futurity*, from "The United States Democratic Review," Volume 6, Issue 23, pp. 426-430, 1839

Reiff, Philip, *The Triumph of the Therapeutic: Uses of Faith After Freud*, New York, Harper and Row, 1966.

Rokeach, Milton, *The Nature of Human Values*, New York, Free Press, 1973.

Rudd, Mark, *Unpublished Memoirs* as quoted in "The Weather Underground," 2002 film by Sam Green and Bill Siegel.

Rudd, Mark, *Underground: My Life with SDS and the Weathermen*, Harper and Collins, New York, 2009.

Rykin, Leland, *That Which God Have Lent Thee: The Puritans and Money*, http://www.apuritansmind.com/

Sageman, Marc, *Understanding Terror Networks*, Philadelphia, University of Pennsylvania Press, 2004.

Sartres, Jean Paul, *Sketch For A Theory of Emotions*, London, Methuen & Co., 1962.

Saver, Jeffrey and John Rabin, *The Neural Substrates of Religious Experience* in "The Journal of Neuropsychiatry," Vol 9, p 498, 1997.

Saul, John Ralston, *On Equilibrium*, New York, Penguin, 2001.

Sacks, Jonathan, *The Dignity of Difference*, London, Continuum, 2002.

Sontag, Susan, *Against Interpretation and Other Essays*, New York, Picador, 1961.

Stark, Rodney, *The Rise of Christianity*, New Jersey, Princeton University Press, 1996.

Storr, Antony, *Feet of Clay*, London, Harper Collins, 1997.

Strongman, K.T., *The Psychology of Emotion*, New York, Wiley and Sons, 1978.

Trungpa, Chogyam, *Cutting Through Spiritual Materialism*, Boston, Shambala, 1973.

Turner, Frederick Jackson, *The Frontier in American History*, New York, Henry Holt, 1921.

Volkin, Vamik, *Blind Trust: Large Groups and Their Leaders in Times of Crises and Terror*, Charlottesville, Pitchstone Publishing, 2004.

Washington, Peter, Madame Blavatsky's Baboon, New York, Schocken Books, 1995.

Washburn, Michael, *The ego and the dynamic ground: A transpersonal theory of human development*, Albany, State University of New York Press, 1995.

Weber, Max, *The Sociology of Charismatic Authority* in "From Max Weber: Essays in Sociology," Ed. Gerth, H.H.and Mills, C. Wright, New York, Oxford U. Press, 1946.

Webster, Richard, *The Body Politic and the Politics of the Body*, <www.richardwebster.net/print/xthepoliticsofthebody.htm>

Wells, H.G., *The Executive Ventures Group Book of Readings*, Denver, in-house publication, 1986.

Wellwood, John, *Awakening The Heart*, Berkeley, Shambala Books, 1983.

Wesley, Michael, *The Search For Moral Authority* in "Griffith Journal," Spring, 2004.

White, Michael and Epston, David, *Narrative Means to Therapeutic Ends*, New York, W.W. Norton, 1990.

Wilber, Ken, *The Pre-Trans Fallacy* in "ReVision," Vol.3, No. 2, 1980.

Wolfe, Tom, *The Me Decade and the Third Great Awakening* in "New York Magazine," August 23, 1976.

Yates, W.B, edited Erdman *The Second Coming* in The Complete Poetry and Prose of William Yates, Berkeley, U. of California Press, 2008.

Zimbardo, Philip and W.C. Banks, C. Haney, *A Study of Prisoners and Guards in a Simulated Prison* in "Naval Research Review," 30, 4-17, 1973.

Zimbardo, Philip and Robert Vallone, *Persuasion, Coercion, and Mind Control*, Lexington, Ginn Custom Publishing, 1983.

Zimbardo, Philip, *The Lucifer Effect*, New York, Random House, 2007.